Laud Humphreys

Laud Humphreys

*Prophet of Homosexuality
and Sociology*

John F. Galliher,
Wayne H. Brekhus, and
David P. Keys

THE UNIVERSITY OF WISCONSIN PRESS

The University of Wisconsin Press
1930 Monroe Street
Madison, Wisconsin 53711

www.wisc.edu/wisconsinpress/

3 Henrietta Street
London WC2E 8LU, England

1   3   5   4   2

Printed in the United States of America

Library of Congress Cataloging-in-Publication Data
Galliher, John F.
Laud Humphreys : prophet of homosexuality and sociology /
John F. Galliher, Wayne Brekhus, David P. Keys.
p. cm.
Includes bibliographical references and index.
ISBN 0-299-20310-7 (hardcover : alk. paper)
ISBN 0-299-20314-x (pbk. : alk. paper)
1. Humphreys, Laud.   2. Sociologists—United States—Biography.
3. Homosexuality—United States.   4. Sociology—Research—Methodology.
I. Brekhus, Wayne.   II. Keys, David Patrick, 1955- .   III. Title.
HM479.H86G35   2004
301′.092—dc22   2004007795

To Lily

Contents

Acknowledgments

The authors gratefully recognize the assistance of Clair Beller Humphreys, David Humphreys, Brian Miller, Donald Granberg, Ronald Farrell, Carole Case, Martin Weinberg, Nancy Turner Myers, Sarah Boggs, PJ McGann, Robert Habenstein, Glenn Goodwin, Fred Lynch, David Pittman, John Hollister, Irving Louis Horowitz, William Yancy, James Henslin, Lee Rainwater, Dusky Lee Smith, Joseph Carrier, John Mitchell, Susanne Carter, and all those interviewed in the course of the research for this book.

Prologue

In September 1967 I joined the University of Missouri–Columbia Department of Sociology as an assistant professor. Having also joined the Episcopal Church that year, I immediately began to hear about an outspoken priest in the church who was forced out of several clergy positions because of his strident support for the Civil Rights movement. Soon thereafter I learned that this man was Laud Humphreys and that he had left the active priesthood and was a graduate student at nearby Washington University in St. Louis. We soon met and became friends. I always found his life to be a mixture of myth and fact, and this book is an attempt to separate the two.

J.F.G.

Laud Humphreys

Introduction

The justification for this book is unusual. Biographies of academics typically include only the most prominent faculty at the most illustrious universities. This biography, however, deals with a social scientist who wrote just a single research monograph, one short textbook, and a handful of journal articles. He was active in social science research for just over a decade. He taught only briefly at one of America's most prestigious research universities.

At first glance this may not appear to be the kind of record that merits a biography, yet it is precisely because Laud Humphreys has had such a large impact on the collective memory of sociology with just a single research manuscript that his career merits renewed interest. It is his controversial dissertation that was published as the book *Tearoom Trade* that makes him noteworthy. This manuscript, written well over thirty years ago, has led to a discourse on professional ethics that continues to this day. That Humphreys never duplicated the tremendous impact of *Tearoom Trade* in any of his other writings adds to the mystique of his career. He was, in common parlance, a "one-hit wonder."

Laud Humphreys's career rose and fell quickly, but his impact on the collective memory and practice of sociology has endured. One anonymous reviewer noted that his career is important in great part because he has become a symbolic representation of broader social movements. This symbolic representation is significant in the Peace and Civil Rights movements, and especially the Gay Liberation movement, as well as serving as an anchor in the increased attention to the rights of human subjects used in research. The irony is that while those who associate his name with civil rights view Humphreys as the epitome of valor and wisdom, many individuals who are concerned with the mistreatment of

3

human subjects characterize his work as the personification of unethical research practice. It is important to keep this uppermost in our minds to avoid replacing biography with iconography.

We hope that this biography, which draws on both primary and secondary data (see Appendix E), sharpens this discourse on professional ethics in the social sciences. We also hope that it revives *Tearoom Trade*'s important contributions (often overlooked in ethics debates) and helps to maintain the memory of Laud Humphreys as a champion of civil rights.

Centrality and Marginality

Coser (1971, xix–xx) argues that biographies of scholars must include the "struggles and successes; the influences of . . . family, peers, and superiors; and involvement or lack of involvement in community affairs." Further, intellectual biographies should also consider the "audiences" the scholar addressed and the individual's "social origins" (xx). We will see that Laud Humphreys's origins in rural Depression–era Oklahoma had a lasting imprint on all aspects of his adult life, including the focus of his research and community action.

Coser additionally writes that such intellectual histories must include some conclusions as to whether a scholar was part of the intellectual elite or "an academic outsider" (1971, xx). One difficulty with such evaluations, as Horowitz (1983, 3) notes, is that "sociology lacks a consensus about who the important figures are." In spite of the cautionary note from Horowitz, an early and anonymous reviewer of this biography wrote: "In all frankness, few people are so important or have led so productive a life as to warrant the writing of a biography about them." This reviewer reflects the standard judgment in such matters that a biography's importance is directly correlated with the professional prestige of the person being considered. Biographies are typically written about widely published professors at prominent universities with many high quality graduate students (Galliher and Galliher 1995). The names of such heroic sociologists include Talcott Parsons, Robert Merton, and James Coleman. All these men have been the subjects of biographies in recent years—Parsons (Gerhardt 1993), Merton (Clark, Modgil, and Modgil 1990), and Coleman (Clark 1996).

Yet if one writes only about the most prominent sociologists it can be argued that one tends to learn the least since there is little about the famous in academia that is not already known. Their lives are already heavily articulated and well documented. The leaders of our profession lead very public lives; their books, articles, departments, and professional offices are part of our disciplinary legend. Moreover, it is a mistake to assume that we gain the most knowledge about a discipline and its institutional culture by studying the most universally and unambiguously successful members.

Just as historians have discovered that knowledge of less successful and marginal people is vital to our understanding of history and culture, the study of marginal and even trouble-making academics is necessary to our understanding of the institutional history and culture of both academia and professional sociology. Remembering Coser's admonitions, surely the "struggles and successes" of the most prominent sociologists will be different than those of others. For example, the requirements for promotion and tenure at one of the nation's leading research universities clearly involve different types of production than elsewhere. There may also be different involvement with "peers and superiors," and, in many cases, prominent family connections facilitate employment in elite universities.

In addition, the involvement in "community affairs" may also be quite different for academic leaders. The involvement of the academic elite in the community is more likely to be at the highest levels of business and government. There is the example of Parsons's service to the U.S. government during World War II (Gerhardt 1993) as well as the work of James S. Coleman (Clark 1996). One interpretation of Coleman's involvement with government is that during the 1960s, when it appeared that the federal leadership supported integration of public schools, Coleman authored a federal report touting the benefits of racial integration in the schools. By the 1970s, however, when federal leadership on integration began to wane, Coleman now purported to find only negative consequences from such racial integration (Galliher and Galliher 1995).

Responding to this kind of behavior from the elites of the discipline with a bit of hyperbole during the American Sociological Association's Annual Meetings, Martin Nicolaus (1969, 155) claimed that "this assembly here tonight is a kind of lie. It is not a coming together of those who study and know, or promote study and knowledge of, social reality. . . . The eyes of sociologists, with few but honorable exceptions, have been turned downwards, and their palms upwards. . . . Eyes down, to study the activities of the lower classes, of the subject population . . . to give information and advice to the ruling class of this society about ways and means to keep the people *down*." While Nicolaus seems to exaggerate the degree to which elite sociologists cater to the powerful, his criticism of the discipline's elites nonetheless hints at the gap between the few prominent sociologists who have the ears of policy makers and those sociologists who do not. Certainly Humphreys's antiestablishment attacks and his controversial methods stand in stark contrast to the safer methods of compromising with established institutions practiced by disciplinary elites.

Study of elite sociologists requires the same justification as one might use in studying kings, presidents, generals, business leaders, or any of the dead white male leaders of Europe. This idea that great men should be studied leaves the vast majority of social life as terra incognita. Social historians now recognize that it is important to go beyond the most successful to the study of ordinary and marginal people. By the same token, we must move beyond the most successful sociologists to those whose success was short-lived and ambiguous, and whose position in the discipline is contested. There are empirical benefits from studying those who challenge the discipline's boundaries and clash with, rather than become part of, its leadership. Studies of the established greats like Parsons, Merton, and Coleman do not yield such insights, for these men did not violate social boundaries.

We can look at where and why Laud Humphreys was marginalized to increase our understanding of the symbolic and moral boundaries in sociology and in academia as a whole. Durkheim (1964) has demonstrated that punishment is a means of social control and also a primary means of maintaining the social boundaries in groups. Those who deviate from the norms are punished either by expulsion from the group or by being relegated to a low social rank (Dentler and Erikson 1959). This can instruct us as to how the profession is organized to discourage and punish certain behaviors. Only by studying marginalized sociologists can we begin to see how the boundaries of the discipline are maintained. Our analysis will demonstrate that Humphreys was marginalized along the following five dimensions: (1) subject matter (2) orientation toward social change (3) ascribed status (4) choice of audiences, and (5) personal behavior.

Subject Matter

Laud Humphreys's focus on the topic of homosexual sex involving men having orgasms in public restrooms was triply marginalized. He was marginalized because of his sympathetic study of devalued men, because he recorded their otherwise intimate sexual behavior, and also because he observed behavior that was at the time categorized as "criminal sodomy" and also a violation of legal statutes prohibiting sexual relations in public. Indeed, the controversy his research methods generated probably had as much to do with what he studied as with how he studied it. His choice of homosexual sex in restrooms as a legitimate site of study no doubt caused greater scrutiny of his methods than other less salacious or controversial topics would have.

Studies of sexual deviance often stain the researcher with the "courtesy stigma" of the population studied (Goffman 1963, 30-31) in a way that studies of poverty do not. The underlying assumption is that the researcher must have more than an intellectual interest in sexuality studies. As such, Taylor and Raeburn (1995) view the study of homosexuality as "high-risk activism" because the researcher is likely to be "outed" as "homosexual" himself. And Chauncey (2000, 300-301) has observed: "As recently as the late 1970s, much of the (relatively small amount of) gay studies work being published was still produced by nonacademics. . . . [M]ost gay academics remained too afraid of the all too real professional consequences of conducting such studies to follow the lead of community-based scholars. . . . The police weren't arresting gay academics anymore, . . . but the climate of fear was so pervasive and powerful as recently as the 1980s." This is magnified when the conduct under study is itself of an explicitly sexual nature. It is one thing to study how gay men negotiate an identity but quite another to study gay and heterosexually married men actually engaging in homosexual behavior, especially when that behavior is categorized as sodomy and prohibited by criminal law.

In a similar manner Alfred Lindesmith's fieldwork among drug addicts beginning in the 1930s marginalized him (Keys and Galliher 2000). Lindesmith was studying a group of people who were largely unknown or devalued and who were routinely engaged in criminal behavior. Early on, this brought Lindesmith to the attention of law enforcement authorities who attempted to suppress his research and publication, and even attempted to have him fired from his university teaching position. The parallels between Humphreys and Lindesmith are instructive to the boundaries of sociology. Both men studied the kinds of deviant behavior that may stain one with the courtesy stigma of one's subjects. Their marginalization was further enhanced by the fact that both men also advocated policy changes that would benefit the stigmatized groups that they studied.

Orientation toward Social Change

Sociologists' attitudes toward social change are other sources of professional marginality. Although sociology is regarded as a liberal discipline,
there is a tempering of activist agendas. Regarding Laud Humphreys,
Horowitz (2001) has observed: "To put matters bluntly, he wrote an
outstanding albeit troubling dissertation—[but] there was no follow-
up. Rather Humphreys took it upon himself to champion the cause of
homosexuality as partisan and participant." According to this reasoning
one must choose between being a serious scholar or a committed activist. This reasoning reflects the general discomfort many in academia
have with individuals combining their scholarship with activism. Lindesmith argued forcefully for rational social changes in U.S. drug laws
that many of his colleagues undoubtedly felt was ill advised (Keys and
Galliher 2000). Certainly during the 1940s and 1950s no one in the discipline joined in his crusade.

Another prime example of an activist scholar is found in Irwin
Deutscher. While a graduate student in sociology at the University of
Missouri, Deutscher was involved in many acts of nonviolent civil dis-
obedience while attempting to racially integrate legally segregated restaurants (Deutscher and Deutscher 1955). These acts included sit-ins at
segregated lunch counters. Deutscher would later become a tenured
professor at Syracuse University. After having been arrested on several
occasions for civil rights protests, the university president summarily
cut his salary in half, thereby forcing him to leave the university.

Activism can be even more costly and more marginalizing to one's
career when it is coupled with possessing an already potentially discred-
iting minority-ascribed status. Minority academics are often faced with
additional barriers to being taken seriously as scholars. Some choose to
downplay their identity in an attempt to fit in, whereas others choose to
embrace the minority label and carve out a somewhat marginalized
niche in the discipline. Humphreys practiced elements of both strategies but increasingly employed the latter and likely suffered in professional prestige as a result of not only being a "partisan" for the gay community but also a "participant" in homosexuality.

Ascribed Status, Professional Marginalization

Race

Oliver Cox was an African American sociologist who, in spite of an im-
pressive record of publication, never held a position at a predominantly

white institution, and his work was never integrated into mainstream sociological writing. Cox was marginalized not only by his race but also by his insistence on using Marxist analysis. He therefore spent most of his career at the predominantly black school Lincoln University in Jefferson City, Missouri (Hunter and Abraham 1987). A white colleague, sociologist Noel Gist, invited Professor Cox to speak on the University of Missouri campus during the McCarthy era in the early 1950s. Professor Cox told his totally white audience that the only means of attaining racial justice in America was a violent Marxist-style revolution. This created a very negative reaction from the University of Missouri administration. Apparently it was one thing to advocate this idea to black students but an entirely different matter to discuss it in front of white students.

Gender

"[Jesse Bernard's] self-image as 'marginal man' nonetheless contained an important truth: as a woman she had been taken less seriously, but for this reason was less worried that inconsistency might somehow damage her career. Whatever the issue was, as she once put it, she could 'get away with it'" (Bannister 1991, 125–26). If Jesse Bernard was given special latitude on the basis of gender, University of Chicago sociologist Jane Addams, earlier in the century, was not. Addams was one of the most important intellectuals of the twentieth century. Beginning her career in the 1890s Addams was generally accepted on her merits for more than two decades. However, during World War I, because of her pacifism, she was ostracized by her colleagues and "targeted by the U.S. government as the most dangerous woman in America" (Deegan 1988, 7). Moreover, in a sweeping move in 1920 all the women in the sociology department at the University of Chicago were transferred to social work.

Age

Robert Park worked as a journalist for much of his adult life and did not begin a career as a sociologist until the age of fifty (Coser 1971). Humphreys also had a prior career and entered sociology only in middle age. The typical punishment for a late arrival in the profession involves severe limits on one's career opportunities. If Laud was to make his mark on the discipline he had to hit the ground running, which he did.

Homosexuality

Finally, Laud Humphreys was an openly gay man, perhaps the first gay sociologist to come out of the closet. And like Cox and Addams before him, his political views and activities were generally not acceptable to the legal and academic authorities.

Audiences

Sociologists assume that audiences, or environments, influence all human experience. There is no reason to assume that it is otherwise for sociologists themselves. During the nineteenth and early twentieth centuries the educated public was a significant consumer of social science books and public lectures. *The Lonely Crowd* (Reisman, Glazer, and Denney 1961) and *Middletown* (Lynd and Lynd 1929) are the best-known illustrations. Recent examples are more difficult to locate, but three stand out: *Habits of the Heart* (Bellah et al. 1985), *The Truly Disadvantaged* (Wilson 1987), and *When Work Disappears* (Wilson 1996).

Catering to a general audience, however, has often been accompanied by professional marginalization. Betty and Al Lee were inclined to public audiences that appeared to guarantee their relegation to low-prestige academic positions. In fact, Betty never held a tenure-track position, and Al (in spite of a massive research output) spent most of his career at Brooklyn College. Al was an expert witness in the U.S. Supreme Court *Brown vs. Topeka School Board* case along with famous psychologist Kenneth Clark. Betty and Al were involved with the Institute for Propaganda Analysis in publicly debunking racism such as spouted by radio priest Fr. Charles Coughlin (Galliher and Galliher 1995).

Sociologist Alfred Lindesmith also devoted most of his long career to the public interest (Keys and Galliher 2000). He championed the reform of U.S. drug policy. He was an avid writer of newspaper and popular magazine articles. He also spent his entire academic career in a confrontation with national drug-control officials. One major dispute involved the American censorship of a film produced by the Canadian government that portrayed drug addicts as both sick and harmless individuals and drug prohibitions as morally wrong. There is little doubt that insistence on communicating with a public audience seriously marginalizes any academic career. We will show that the frequent use of *Tearoom Trade* by ethnographers, its significance for emerging queer theory, and its frequent mention in introductions to sociology textbooks leaves no doubt that Humphreys's book has captured diverse audiences. Certainly his work in the ministry influenced his inclination to address a broad public audience. Ironically the frequent scolding given to him in introductory sociology textbooks surely captures the attention of some of the public.

Personal Misbehavior

Alfred McClung Lee caused his share of conflict. He waged a public dispute with James Coleman over the latter's criticism of integrated public schools. Many in the discipline felt that this criticism reflected Lee's bad manners, sour disposition, and lack of respect for academic freedom. In addition, Lee was an autocrat as department chair at Brooklyn College (Galliher and Galliher 1995). C. Wright Mills was notorious for political infighting with his colleagues (Horowitz 1983). Thorstein Veblen began his higher education at Carleton College, an institution he thoroughly disliked. He only respected one faculty member, who, as it happens, was known for his socialist leanings. Veblen created a major stir on campus by delivering a paper to an assembly of faculty and students on "A Plea for Cannibalism" (Coser 1971, 277). Later, at the University of Chicago, his dismal teaching, libertine sexual practices, radical politics, and disdain for colleagues led to his dismissal (Coser 1971). This same pattern of behavior led to only relatively brief appointments at Stanford and the University of Missouri. Similarly L. L. Bernard had a myriad of battles with departmental colleagues and, moreover, was "a womanizer of almost Olympic stature" (Bannister 1987, 131). He was perpetually on the move from one university to another to escape the problems he had created. The inconsistency is that many male academics have well-earned reputations as womanizers yet seem to have suffered no professional costs for their behavior. Thus it appears that sexual deviance is punished only in those instances where the individual is additionally marginalized for other reasons. We will see that Humphreys was difficult as a colleague, teacher, husband, and father. Moreover, he left his wife and children to live with a man.

Methods: Insider versus Outsider Perspectives

Teaching and research in sociology until the 1960s generally involved white men who could become experts on people of color and the poor because white men were perceived as the embodiment of "objective neutrality." William F. Whyte had conducted fieldwork among young men in an Italian American slum (1955), and Liebow (1967) had done fieldwork among lower-class African Americans. Whyte and Liebow were white professional men studying lower-class people. White men routinely taught courses on race relations and African Americans. The beginning of the end of this trend is found in Becker's (1963) study of dance band musicians while working as a musician. Becker studied fellow jazz musicians, and shortly thereafter Humphreys studied men involved in homosexual sex in public toilets (1970a).

Prior to Becker's and Humphreys's research it had generally been assumed that the fieldworker must study those who were different in order to maintain objectivity. Gary Marx recalled that during the late 1960s he was widely regarded as a leading expert on race relations in America. By the early 1970s "whites writing about minority groups and favoring integration came under increased attack from segments of the left and the right" (Marx 1990, 265). Since the 1970s it has generally been assumed that sharing a perspective with one's subjects is a positive and not a negative factor. To demonstrate Laud Humphreys's lasting significance, the concluding chapter of this book explores the impact of his work on related ethical and legal standards in social science research.

Methodological Traps in Biographical Research

An anonymous reviewer wrote: "Biographies are inherently subjective works and as such they tend to be less objective than other scholastic genres. Biographies in general, and academic ones in particular, tend to either libel or lionize their subjects." This is not necessarily true. Horowitz (1983) demonstrates that while Mills was a man with great intellectual gifts, he was still flawed. Mills could be arrogant and always took criticism personally. Old friends became enemies if they dared to criticize his work. Galliher and Galliher (1995) show that Al Lee, while a passionate champion of human rights, was at times far from being democratic and seldom attempted to understand those who disagreed with him. During the early 1950s, while he chaired the sociology department at Brooklyn College, Lee demanded that the department hire a Japanese American woman who had been imprisoned in a U.S. internment camp throughout World War II. He refused to allow his colleagues to consider other candidates. Here we will attempt to tell all sides of the story of Laud Humphreys.

1

Birth and Beginnings

Just as Coser (1971) imagined, the influence of Laud Humphreys's family was of great importance in his life. Robert Allan (Laud) Humphreys was born on October 16, 1930, in Chickasha, Oklahoma, to Ira Denver Humphreys and Stella Bernice Humphreys. Laud had two brothers—William of Oklahoma City (who was ten years his senior) and Howard of Kent, Washington (twenty years older) (*Claremont Courier* 1988). According to Laud's daughter, Clair, his brothers were distant even prior to his coming out as gay. Thereafter they were hostile. Clair said that she only saw one brother (Howard) once, for approximately an hour, when he was passing through Los Angeles.

For his part, Laud had hardly anything positive to say about his father, who served as a Democrat in the Oklahoma House of Representatives from 1951 to 1953 representing Grady County, except that he sponsored legislation making the show tune *Oklahoma* the official state song. He died on November 18, 1953, while serving a second term as House representative. His obituary in the *Daily Oklahoman* (1953, 1) notes that he was a "retired wire chief of Southwestern Bell Telephone Co. Survivors include three sons." Laud also recalled that, "as a state legislator, my father was most diligent in promoting the passage of Sunday 'blue laws.' He also helped establish a law school in the attic of the State Capitol so that blacks would not have to be admitted to the University" (Humphreys 1975, 229). Referring to his own imprisonment for destruction of federal property during a demonstration against the Vietnam War, Laud noted, "I am one of those people who have been officially 'rehabilitated' by months in jail and years on probation, yet I still have utter contempt for a number of statutes on the law books" (Humphreys 1975, 229), emphasizing the repressive bills sponsored by his father.

13

At the time of his father's death, Laud wrote a long, melancholy letter to him retained in his files at the time of his own death (Humphreys, n.d.). It reads in part: "I regret that you and I never shared the two great secrets that kept us from being really close to each other. You see I never told you that I was gay." Laud went on to explain that he learned that his father was gay immediately after his funeral. "I remember that you went off alone to the Mardi Gras every year and now I understand why." Laud also noted in the letter that he had written to his brothers three years earlier to tell them he was gay and had had no contact with them since. He closed by saying: "I love you and still miss you. Please send me your love too." From his records, and from his family and friends, we are left with no accounts of his mother, who died on June 6, 1946, when Laud was fifteen years old.

Education

In 1948 Laud graduated from Chickasha High School in Oklahoma. His undergraduate education included a year at the University of Virginia, 1948-49. He then attended Colorado College, graduating in 1952. While at Colorado College he worked as a reporter for the *Colorado Springs Free Press*. Both these institutions, although not truly elite, are relatively expensive. This, together with Laud's father's membership in the state legislature, demonstrates that as a boy he was probably accustomed to a comfortable standard of living.

Laud graduated from Seabury–Western Episcopal Theological Seminary in 1955. A fellow Episcopalian clergyman recalled Laud's early years immediately after seminary: "I met him in 1955 at a clergy meeting in Oklahoma City. Laud had been reared as a Methodist but wanted to leave all that behind him. He wanted to be baptized again, and was baptized again in 1955, to make a new start in the faith. He took the name Laud after an Anglican Church leader, William Laud" (Jones 2001).

William Laud became the Chancellor of Oxford University in 1629 and did a great deal to encourage scholars (*Oxford Dictionary of the Christian Church* 1974). In 1633 he became the Archbishop of Canterbury and, in spite of his lofty post, was "compassionate in his defense of the rights of the common people against landowners" (*Lesser Feasts and Fasts* 2001), but he was ultimately executed in 1645 for his demands for liturgical uniformity. So the role model important to Laud Humphreys was a man who valued scholarship and the Anglican liturgy, who was compassionate toward the poor, and who ultimately lost his life on the basis of principle. At the time of his 1955 baptism Mary Ann Ledbetter of Oklahoma City was Laud's Godmother, and she "indeed [was] like a mother to him" (Jones 2001).

One of Laud's fellow students in seminary said: "We were roommates for two years at Seabury—the 'Middler' year and senior year—he was a good student but had trouble with Greek" (Rhudy 2001). Laud attended Washington University from 1965 to 1968 and in the latter year received a Ph.D. Perhaps recognizing his problems with foreign languages he began taking German and French in the summer session. He subsequently took nine hours of graduate-level anthropology and sociology during the fall 1965 and spring 1966 semesters, and the next school year he took twelve hours each semester, including three hours of Field Research each term. He took an additional three hours of Field Research in the summer of 1967. During the fall 1967 semester he took nine hours of Independent Work and three hours of Field Research, and, finally, during the spring 1968 semester he took twelve hours of Independent Work. Laud breezed through the graduate program, earning a masters and Ph.D. degree in just less than three years. He was admitted to Ph.D. candidacy in April 1965, awarded the MA degree (without thesis) in June 1967, and passed the preliminary examination in September 1967. His dissertation was accepted and his oral exam passed in May 1968; his Ph.D. degree was conferred in June 1968.

Wife and Children

Laud was married to Nancy Margaret Wallace on October 1, 1960. The couple divorced in 1980. Nancy was born on October 23, 1933. She graduated from the University of Tulsa and, at the time of her wedding, was recognized as belonging to Tulsa society as a member of the Tulsa Junior League. Prior to her wedding to Laud, the Tulsa social scene was abuzz with anticipation. A *Tulsa Tribune* headline (1960) noted "Parties Continue for Miss Nancy Wallace." These articles noted that she was a member of the Kappa Kappa Gamma sorority and that her fiancé was a member of Beta Theta Pi, a prominent social fraternity. Cards and notes from Laud that Nancy saved in her engagement album demonstrate his deep love for her.

One of Laud's clergy friends recalled: "I was shocked when Laud told me he wanted to marry her because I knew he was gay. At this point his explanation was that he was actually bisexual. In any event, they had a big church wedding in Trinity Church in Tulsa" (Jones

2001). Another friend remembered: "Nancy helped him in everything, including counseling draft dodgers at Southern Illinois University" (Rhudy 2001).

Friends recalled: "Nancy was from Tulsa and was interested in community theatre, was flamboyant, dramatic and positive. She was like Auntie Mame" (Jones 2001). "Nancy was a tall, lean and pretty woman—Kathryn Hepburnish in terms of demeanor. She was charming, gracious and always spoke with grand gestures" (Schwartz 2001). Nancy's daughter, Clair (Beller 2001), remembered that her mother "was quite an accomplished actress in high school, college and for several years after our [me and my brother's] birth. She loved classical music, books, sewing and the performing arts. . . . My mother had a very dramatic personality. She seemed to enter a room and everyone knew she had arrived, possibly the theatre training!" Ann Stromberg (2001), one of Laud's colleagues in sociology, remembers Nancy as "warm, flexible and uncomplaining in spite of her tremendous health problems. She was a deeply spiritual person, who was a devoted mother and who was always active in the local Episcopal Church. When I arrived at Pitzer in 1973 I was alone, and Laud and Nancy made a special point of inviting me to their home for Thanksgiving and other occasions."

Nancy and Laud adopted two infants, a daughter, Clair Elizabeth, and a son, David Wallace. Clair was born on November 15, 1963, in Kansas City, Kansas, and David on August 28, 1964, in Guthrie, Oklahoma. Laud's clergy friends, Rob Rhudy and Vern Jones, were chosen to be David's Godparents (Jones 2001).

After a long struggle with diabetes, Nancy died on December 8, 1991 (Beller 2001). Clair recalled that Nancy had diabetes since the age of ten. Nancy's mother was a Christian Scientist, and thus Nancy had had no appropriate medical treatment until she left home, seriously compounding her health problems as an adult.

Early Church Posts and Civil Rights Activism

After graduating from the seminary Laud had several relatively brief clergy appointments. The first year out of the seminary he and two other priests (Rob Rhudy and Charles Sutton) shared a salary and a half by living together in Woodward, Oklahoma, where they conducted morning prayer, mass, and daily evening prayer. Then on the weekends Laud would go to Guymon, Oklahoma (121 miles west of Woodward), to spend Saturday and Sunday serving St. Stephen's mission (Jones

2003). Laud did this 1955–1956, moving to Cripple Creek, Colorado (1956–59), to Bartlesville, Oklahoma (1959–61), to Guthrie, Oklahoma (1961–63), and to Wichita, Kansas (1963–65) (*Episcopal Clerical Directory* 1999). In the early 1980s he was very angry with the church, but, a few months prior to his death, he again began to work in the church, specifically St. Thomas Church in Hollywood (Jones 2001). The church secretary remembered meeting Laud just months before his death on August 22, 1988. Church records indicate that Laud first celebrated the Eucharist there in September 1987 and that his last Eucharist was in April 1988.

An old friend from his days in Wichita recalled that Laud once told him that, in Guthrie, "his and Nancy's clothes and other belongings were destroyed and the house ransacked by members of the vestry. He then went to a very affluent parish, St. James in Wichita, Kansas. Here he was an assistant pastor and in that capacity had started an adult education program on racism in the U.S. I was teaching at Wichita State University at the time (1964) and Laud asked me to come in to teach as a part of this program. That is when I first met him" (Mitchell 2001).

Laud remembered those experiences clearly: In 1964 "I was four years into the civil rights movement then and about to be fired from my pastorate for preaching a sermon entitled 'Selma, Alabama: Two Thousand Years of Christian Failure.' The summer of 1965 I went to Mississippi and found that civil rights had become black freedom" (Humphreys 1972b, x). "Laud saw everything in superlatives—the least, best or worst were the words he typically used. Laud was a very passionate person. But Laud's sermons put the St. James' Rector Joe Young on the spot with his wealthy congregation. Laud gave extreme sermons with themes such as 'If you don't do anything about poverty you are living in sin,' using Matthew 25 as his text" (Rhudy 2001). Here the words of Jesus read in part: "Depart from me, you cursed, into the eternal fire . . . for I was hungry and you gave me no food, I was thirsty and you gave me no drink, I was a stranger and you did not welcome me, naked and you did not clothe me, sick and in prison and you did not visit me. . . . Truly, I say to you, as you did it not to one of the least of these, you did it not to me. And [you] will go away into eternal punishment."

Sociologist Dusky Lee Smith (2001) recalled that several of his relatives were members of the Episcopal Church in Guthrie, including his uncle, his aunt, two cousins, and their husbands. "I had already moved away from Guthrie and did not know Laud, but during a visit home three of my family members told me that they were appalled once they realized that Laud 'was a nigger lover and a Commie.'" Apparently Laud had visited the nearby all-black institution, Langston College, and had invited the students to come to the Episcopal Church. "My cousins and an aunt were terribly upset that Laud had invited 'niggers' to come to the church. My aunt complained that 'this nigger came right out to the pulpit. I didn't know what to think. Then during communion here came the nigger-black fingers with the white wafers.'"

Smith continued (2001): "In any case, the husbands of my cousins felt that an awful situation had developed at the church. They decided that they should go to the priest's house next to the church and confront Laud. Nancy, who was pregnant at the time, opened the front door but the screen door was latched. When the two men demanded to see Laud she refused to let them in, saying he was not available. One of my cousins broke through the screen door and Nancy fell to the floor. The two men entered Laud's office looking for 'Communist' books and pulled several to the floor. They rifled through his desk and files, throwing many of his papers in the air." It is worth noting that Nancy never bore any children thereafter.

Laud's friend, John Mitchell (2001) also recalled: "After he was fired from St. James he told me he was going to Washington University to study toward a Ph.D. We discussed a dissertation in sociology about the members of the Mattachine Society (an early secret organization for homosexuals) written by a woman who was a student at Missouri University." Using anonymous questionnaires this woman found, consistent with the stereotypic Freudian pattern, that men with strong mothers and weak fathers were more likely than others to develop into adult homosexuals (Mathes 1966). "Laud felt that she had erred by using only questionnaire data. To understand gay people Laud felt it was essential to collect direct observational data, which he early on intended to do" (Mitchell 2001).

2

Becoming an Instant Icon

It is now central to sociology's disciplinary folklore that Alvin Gouldner physically assaulted Laud in 1968. Gouldner sought revenge after finding an unflattering caricature of him on the Washington University sociology department bulletin board. He imagined that Laud had penned it because it was accompanied by Latin phrases, and he knew that Laud had been trained as a priest (Yancy 2001a). The format for these posters was taken from the *Ramparts* magazine series "Sorel's Bestiary," which featured some prominent figure depicted in nonhuman form such as a wild animal, fish, or bird, together with a pseudo-Latin name. For example, the cover of the July 1966 issue featured President Lyndon Johnson as a bird with the name "Hawkus Caucus Americanus."

Actually Laud had placed other unflattering likenesses of Gouldner on the walls of the building, for example, a "Wanted" poster featuring a suspect with red hair and very large ears (Henslin 2001b). After several pictures of this nature had appeared overnight in the sociology building Gouldner went to Laud's office on the third floor of McMillan Hall, where the department's graduate student offices were housed. Gouldner approached Laud while extending his hand. Laud reported that he imagined that Gouldner wanted to shake hands and make up. Instead, Gouldner hit him in the face, knocking him down and then kicking him (Henslin 2001b). Typed notes in Laud's files indicated that Gouldner said: "If you ever mention my name in public again, I'll kill you." Henslin recalled that soon afterward he "saw Laud leaving McMillan Hall, crying. I could see footprints on his pants. I took him to the campus infirmary." A copy of one of these posters was found in Laud's private files (see Appendix C). The copy of the poster has a handwritten note indicating that it had been obtained from the files of Professor Lee

Rainwater, who was Laud's adviser, leaving some doubt about Laud's authorship. Yet Gouldner understandably assumed that Laud had been the author since Laud was a leading student activist. A February 1968 photograph (*Student Life* 1968a) of Laud in the student newspaper shows him leading a group of protestors in front of the campus placement office, where a representative of Dow Chemical was scheduled to hold job interviews.

Some representatives of the Sociology Graduate Student Union had this view of the posters (Washington University 1968a): "These notices have been seriously disruptive to our common academic endeavors." In an undated memo ten graduate students argued that, "the recent incident between a member of the faculty and a student should remain a private matter between the parties involved. It should in no way be made a public issue. And, it certainly should not be made a police issue. The incident was, in our opinion, nowhere near so serious as some persons wish to make it." One member of the Washington University sociology faculty argued that "there were many [other] interpretations— from it being a largely fictive event to little more than pushing and shoving." Contrary to the pleadings of these graduate students this confrontation did become a public issue and, within a month, caused a blip on the national radar screen. On June 10 a *New York Times* (1968, 25) article covered the conflict with the headline "Sociology Professor Accused of Beating Student."

Four senior members of the faculty were so outraged by this confrontation that they wrote to the chancellor of the university asking that Gouldner be suspended from the university faculty and barred from campus (Washington University 1968c). This letter noted that during the prior year Gouldner had "engaged in insulting attacks, both on and off the campus, against his colleagues in the University. His behavior reached a point where it prevented the members of the Department from carrying out their duties of teaching and research." In 1967 Gouldner was given a choice: he could disassociate himself from all participation in the department and, in return, would be given the post of Max Weber Research Professor of Social Theory. He accepted this plan. In 1968, after Gouldner had assaulted Laud, the letter asking that Gouldner be suspended from the faculty and barred from campus noted that Laud would soon receive his Ph.D. and "shortly thereafter will join our faculty" (Washington University 1968c). While Laud never joined the faculty, he did receive a Ph.D. from Washington University in 1968, and his dissertation was published as *Tearoom Trade* in 1970.

Lee Rainwater (2001), who was Laud's dissertation supervisor, recalled, "after Gouldner's attack the university was very upset and tried to make Laud a scapegoat, criticizing his research and arguing that he had not filed the very new human subjects review papers. Fortunately a vice-provost took some responsibility for that, we filed the papers and he got his degree. But while all this was going on he had to work out ways to make sure his records were not subpoenaed. His maturity and self-confidence helped a lot during that time. He took to the literature on deviant behavior with great interest and enthusiasm. He particularly liked Howie Becker's work. He felt this was [one] immediate cause of Gouldner's attack. Gouldner had written an article ['The Sociologist as Partisan' (1968)] in which he attacked Becker and Laud took great exception to it. He had criticized Gouldner, he told me, at a party for his nastiness to Becker in the article and Gouldner heard about it." That this article was of importance to Laud is reflected in the fact that it was one of only a few that remained in his files after his death.

In the midst of all this turmoil it was announced in July 1968 (*St. Louis Globe-Democrat* 1968b) that Washington University would no longer provide financial support for *Trans-action* magazine. In September 1968 the university announced that the magazine was being sold to a corporation headed by Irving Louis Horowitz (Washington University 1968d). Although Alvin Gouldner had been one of the magazine's founders, along with Horowitz and Rainwater, any relationship Gouldner had with the publication was now terminated. Gouldner's honorific title was also temporarily suspended (*Student Life* 1968b). The *St. Louis Globe-Democrat* (1968c) reported, on July 18, that because of the constant furor in the department the Arts and Science Dean had removed the sociology department chair and appointed another without consulting the faculty.

Also in July the *Globe-Democrat* (1968d) reported that, at the request of the university chancellor, the National Institute of Mental Health (NIMH) was sending a team to investigate the sociology department prior to the release of a $1.2 million federal grant to Rainwater. In a memo dated July 31, the team determined that "it is true that nowadays sodomists are rarely if ever prosecuted for this felony, and lookouts or 'watchqueens' probably never. It also may be arguable that if Mr. Humphreys had been charged with a felony, his exclusively 'research' purpose and absence of felonious intent would have resulted in his acquittal" (NIMH 1968). Laud's notes indicated that on June 20, 1968, the chancellor insisted that the university would allow Rainwater to receive the large

NIMH grant only on the condition that Laud would not be employed at the university. A *Globe-Democrat* article on June 12 (1968a) noted that the chancellor had characterized the fight between Gouldner and Humphreys as "infantile." On November 26 Laud wrote to the personnel office at Washington University asking for workmen's compensation for the medical bills incurred as a result of Gouldner's assault (Humphreys 1968b). There is no evidence that the university ever complied.

Looking back on Laud's life it seems clear that his national visibility and career were actually given a boost as a consequence of Alvin Gouldner's assault. Even when only a beginning assistant professor, Laud's name and research had already gained national significance, associated as they were with this conflict with one of the most prominent sociologists of the twentieth century. That many on the faculty at Washington University continued to come into conflict with Gouldner may help to explain why they seemed especially ready, after the confrontation, to rally around Laud and to offer him support.

3

Historical and Intellectual Context of *Tearoom Trade*

The 1960s and Washington University

Laud wrote about the protracted conflict when "the New York City Police raided the Stonewall Inn, an after-hours gay bar on Christopher Street, on [Friday] June 27, 1969" (Humphreys 1972b, 5). "Confrontations with the police continued in the neighborhood for four more nights" (Humphreys 1972b, 6). The gay community was serving notice that never again would it tolerate routine police harassment. The historical and political context of *Tearoom Trade* undoubtedly heightened the awareness and significance of this book. The police had often raided the bar before, but the police were amazed to see that the typical docility of the patrons had unexpectedly turned into white-hot anger. Days of open rebellion ensued that included members of the gay community shouting "Pigs" and "Gestapo" at officers, chasing police officers while threatening to rip off their uniforms, throwing bricks, bottles, and dog feces at officers, and, in one instance, taking a group of them hostage at the bar the police had just raided (Duberman 1993). "The generation of lesbians and gay men galvanized by Stonewall had already witnessed five tumultuous years of intense political activity that fundamentally challenged American values—black civil rights, the student anti-war movement" (Escoffier 1992, 11). Laud participated in all of this. In any case, as Rosenfeld (1998) has noted, the timing of a book's publication makes a great difference in its success. This was clearly true for *Tearoom Trade*, coming out as it did in 1970.

Laud recalled that while he was at Washington University the school was unique: "Now, in such an environment, there are no taboo topics or forbidden strategies" (Humphreys 1975, 218). It was, and is, one of the nation's great research universities. Eminent anthropologist Jules Henry encouraged students' fieldwork demonstrating oppression in the city's schools, and Lee Rainwater did the same in city housing—winning few friends for the faculty among local power elites. Always full of contradictions, Alvin Gouldner encouraged a union among the sociology graduate students, enabling them to press their demands with the faculty and the administration (Yancy 2001b). This was a cutting edge and exciting department at a time that precisely coincided with a sea change in the national gay community. Amid the turmoil of the 1960s this department prided itself on being the leader of graduate sociology programs emphasizing a new and radical tradition. In this environment Laud was the perfect department citizen.

The full extent of the uniqueness of the sociology department at Washington University can be appreciated by comparing it to other graduate departments during the 1960s. At this time most departments were still marked by a good deal of social distance and formality in the relationships between graduate students and faculty. This seems not to have been the case at Washington University. In hindsight some might contend that both the department faculty and the graduate students had the weaknesses of their strengths being as they were a part of a thoroughly democratic group. Because of the informality in this community, this was not an easy group for the administration to control from the top down. Ultimately the university administration had had enough, and the department was closed in 1989.

Rainwater (2001) remembered Laud fondly: "As best I can remember he came to me in his first year as a student to do a reading course in deviant behavior and to work with me on a study of homosexuality. He talked about his work with gay men as a priest in Chicago. (He did not tell me he was gay until some years after he got his degree.) He explored several scenes before settling on the tearoom. He was a very careful and thoughtful field-worker and would have much to discuss and get advice on when we met. Laud was always a pleasure to work with as a student and as a researcher, partly because he was a mature person who brought a lot of experience to his study of sociology."

Rainwater directed Laud's dissertation. Rainwater and David Pittman, who was also on Laud's dissertation committee, published an article in 1967 on professional ethics at the time Laud was collecting his dissertation data. Rainwater and Pittman reported on research in the infamous St. Louis Pruitt–Igoe Housing Project. The housing project was initially occupied in 1954 and became all black almost immediately. There were forty-three eleven-story buildings that by 1967 had 27 percent of its units vacant, the highest in the United States. Rampant crime and a lack of personal safety were the primary causes of these vacancies. The Rainwater and Pittman research, funded by NIMH, was intended to locate the pathological conditions in city housing that were causing these problems.

Rainwater and Pittman (1967, 361) raised the following points emphasizing the rights of the researcher: "Ethics can be seen as also a concern with *our* rights, and an effort to legitimate those rights in the eyes of other institutions and the public" [emphasis added]. Even in the instance of federally funded research, Rainwater and Pittman raised the question of the nature of one's client. They argued that researchers have to answer the question of "exactly the nature of our sponsorship and of who the 'client' [was] to whom we were responsible" (360). Independence from the government is even advised when faced with legal action. "We maintain that, once having given the promise of confidentiality, we have an obligation not to reveal any information we possess which could identify an individual or connect him with what he has told us" (363). If researchers' data have the potential of being subpoenaed, they should "obliterate identifying information on records" (364). Laud learned this lesson well and would soon do precisely this.

If the rights of research sponsors are minimized by Rainwater and Pittman, sensitivity to the rights of individuals and groups who are the subjects of the research is emphasized. "The problem of confidentiality becomes much more complicated when the group one studies is small, and when the individuals in it are necessarily considered responsible for the behavior of all the other members as well as their own. In such a situation there is really no way [to present] findings about the group and at the same time [protect] their identities" (Rainwater and Pittman 1967, 364). Also, "if one describes in full and honest detail behavior which the public will define as immoral, degraded, deviant, and criminal, will not the effect be to damage the very people we hope our study will eventually help?" (361). Some have argued that this applies to the activities in tearooms studied by Humphreys (see, for example, Warwick 1975a).

Rainwater and Pittman encouraged Laud's independence of thought. Merely because the Pruitt–Igoe research was federally funded did not mean that NIMH was a "client" or that the researchers had to jettison their rights as investigators. Thus, according to Rainwater and Pittman, there are at least four interested parties: the individual research subjects, the groups to which the subjects belong, the researcher, and the funding agency. The interests of research subjects are clearly paramount and next come the rights of researchers.

Origins of, and Support for, the Idea of *Tearoom Trade*

The idea of studying homosexual behavior in the community predated Laud Humphreys by approximately three decades. Sometime during the mid-1930s University of Chicago sociology professor Herbert Blumer suggested to his graduate student advisee Alfred Lindesmith that he study homosexual men in Chicago for his dissertation research. Blumer's suggestion was, in turn, almost certainly influenced by the fieldwork of University of Chicago–trained sociologist Nels Anderson, as found in *The Hobo: The Sociology of the Homeless Man* (University of Chicago Press, 1923). Anderson observed that, among homeless men, "homosexual practices arise almost inevitably in . . . situations of sex isolation, [because] debarred from family life, he hungers for intimate associations and affection" (Anderson 1923, 149). In any case, a colleague remembered that "Lindesmith started to pursue this but found the fieldwork too difficult. Striking up relationships with these people was distasteful to him and thus he decided against this course of study. At this point he accepted Blumer's backup plan of studying drug addicts in the community, a topic that would become Lindesmith's life's work" (Schuessler 2001). Had Lindesmith accepted Blumer's initial idea, one may speculate on the course of such research in the 1930s. Certainly, at this early time, such research would have been an exceedingly difficult choice, and it may well have made professional employment for Lindesmith impossible.

In any event, approximately four decades later Laud recalled: "When my first graduate professor, in discussing a proposed research project, urged me to study the gay bars of St. Louis, I took it as a serious challenge. 'Get out of your sheltered tower,' she advised. 'Get out in the streets and get your hands dirty!'" (Humphreys 1975, 223–24). Helen Gouldner (Alvin Gouldner's wife), who was the only woman on the department faculty at the time, recalled that she "often advised students to get out into the real world" (2001). Laud mentioned a deep intellectual debt to his professors: "Lee Rainwater has exercised the greatest influence on this study" (Humphreys 1970a, xvii). He acknowledged other faculty at Washington University—Irving L. Horowitz and David Pittman—as well as support from NIMH for a pre-doctoral fellowship.

Laud's Ph.D. committee included Rainwater, professors Irving Louis Horowitz, Robert Boguslaw, Robert Hamblin, Richard Willis, and Frank Miller (law); associate professors Rodney Coe and Helen Gouldner; as well as one assistant professor, William Yancy (Washington University 1968b). The final examination took place on May 16, 1968. On June 18 the chancellor (Eliot 1968a) wrote to Laud informing him that it appeared that, in his dissertation research, he had failed to follow university regulations and federal law in the protection of human subjects and may also have violated the criminal law of the state of Missouri. "This raises the possibility that the degree may have to be revoked. Accordingly, you would be well advised to refrain from, or at least postpone, the use of the title 'Doctor.'" The chancellor also contacted the Aldine Publishing Company in an attempt to stop the publication process (Eliot 1968c).

On June 21 the sociology department secretary (Brown 1968) took responsibility for failing to submit the proper human subjects' forms for Laud's dissertation. The investigation complete, the chancellor informed Laud on July 1 that he had been cleared of all charges (Eliot 1968b). A *St. Louis Post Dispatch* (1968) article appeared on July 18 which indicated that seven sociologists on the Washington University faculty publicly charged that the university administration had taken "irregular and precipitous actions" against the department. The charges were included in a letter sent to the dean of the College of Arts and Science. The letter alleged that "we are under attack." The department chair had been replaced by summary action of the administration, Rainwater's federal grant had been delayed by the administration, and the legitimacy of Laud's dissertation had been questioned. His publisher had been contacted in an effort to interfere with his book project. The article's headline tells it all: "Eliot Denies Charges by Seven Sociologists."

Laud later recalled: "I started out studying the gay community in St. Louis, but my dissertation adviser wanted me to focus on where the 'average guy' goes to get a blowjob. Once I got started in the subject, I was fascinated. Like most men who are married and closeted—and I was both in those days—my sexual outlets were largely furtive and impersonal. Tearooms held both sexual and intellectual fascination for me" (Miller 1982, 39).

Laud spent ten years in the clergy of the Episcopal Church ministering to the gay community: "From 1955 to 1965, I served parishes in

Oklahoma, Colorado, and Kansas, twice serving as Episcopal campus chaplain on a part-time basis. Because I was considered 'wise' and did not attempt to 'reform' them, hundreds of homosexuals of all sorts and conditions came to me during those years for counseling. Having joined me in counseling parishioners over the coffee pot for many a night, my wife provided much understanding assistance in this area of my ministry" (Humphreys 1970a, 23). Thus the dedication of the book seems entirely fitting: "To my wife Nancy, and my children, Clair and David, whose encouragement and love made this research possible." According to Clair, Nancy had come up with the title for the book.

In the introduction to *Tearoom Trade* Rainwater discussed the *micromanagement of time and space* and that the research uncovered "socially constructed patterns of use of time [and] space" so that "activity in the tearooms is organized to make what is highly stigmatized seem matter of fact and taken for granted" (Humphreys 1970a, viii, x). "Sanitary elimination in parks and . . . [t]he need for covert homosexual gratification, alternate over a period of minutes in an area of a hundred square feet, and yet do not conflict in their everyday operation" (ix).

In chapter 1 of his book Humphreys (1970a, 2) observes that "British slang has used 'tea' to denote 'urine'" and that this may help to explain the origin of the use of tearoom in gay parlance. Chapter 1 also describes the temporal and physical environment of homosexual encounters in public restrooms. Given the anonymity and the impersonality of the sexual liaisons, participants often acquire stronger sentimental attachments to the buildings in which they meet for sexual encounters than to the individuals with whom they have sex. This first chapter explains that there were twelve restrooms in the park where Laud collected his observations. The federal Work Projects Administration built these facilities during the Great Depression of the 1930s. The restrooms are "constructed of a native white stone with men's and women's facilities back-to-back under one red roof [with] heavy wooden doors" shielded from public view by a privacy fence. Each facility has two windows with "opaque glass . . . covered with heavy screen" (4).

In chapter 2 Humphreys discusses his research methods, including passing as a deviant actor to gain access to the setting. He collected observations while serving as a "watchqueen," or a voyeur and lookout for sexual partners (Humphreys 1970a, 26). He was making observations by April 1966 and spent more than two years in the field. Accordingly Laud noted that "the real problem is not one of making contact with the subculture but of making the contact 'stick'" to actually carry out extended research (24). He emphasized that the only way to study highly discreditable behavior without ending the practice being studied is to pose as a "fellow deviant" (25). Using this technique Laud indicated that he "made fifty systematic observations of tearoom encounters, fifty-three acts of fellatio were observed at those times" (12).

Laud's description of the restrooms when compared to photographs we took of the facilities cast some doubt on Laud's description of his research techniques. Laud (1970a, 28) noted: "I was able to move around the room at will, from window to window, and to observe all that went on." However, the windows are small and, as he noted, to ensure privacy are covered with opaque glass as well as metal grillwork. Laud would have had only the slightest view of the approaches even if windows are typically broken as Laud noted.

The interiors of the male restrooms are similar, measuring approximately twenty feet wide by twelve feet deep with three walled compartments: one for urinals, another for the sink, and one for the commode. The interiors appear to be original and show no sign of ever having been electrified. Laud notes that there were no doors on the stalls in these toilets. The exterior doors to the lavatories open inward and again, as Laud has noted, an exterior privacy wall obstructs views. This architecture indicates that Laud probably could not have collected his observations while serving as a watchqueen. He could not have watched from the doorway because his view would have been blocked by the privacy wall—all the more so if he moved into the lavatory to hold open the door. Given the poor interior lighting and the obscured windows and doorways, it would appear that Laud could not have served as a watchqueen while observing the behavior inside. Later accounts have not confirmed any evidence of such a role due to these difficulties of watching for intruders while simultaneously observing action within the restroom (Desroches 1990).

The primary remaining explanation for the richness of the data from his fieldwork is that he was a *participant observer*. Fine (1993) has argued that ethnographers are often confronted with a conflict between institutional values and the realities of what it takes to conduct field research. While Humphreys certainly had to present himself to the discipline as a neutral observer, his involvement may have been more than he was able to report. Any inaccuracies in Laud's reporting in his 1968 dissertation are understandable, since the behavior he described was a criminal offense at the time. An admission to numerous sexual contacts in the St. Louis lavatories would have made him liable to arrest, prosecution, and possibly imprisonment. Such an admission would have probably precluded him from receiving a Ph.D. or a university teaching position. This likely inaccuracy in Laud Humphreys's reporting of his fieldwork methodology, however, should not make us less confident in the quality of his data. Laud may have been even closer to his data than anyone could have imagined. His behavior was his data. Indeed, Fine (1993) also observed that it is not unheard of for ethnographers to become sexually involved with their subjects. Even though "the existence of saucy tales of lurid assignations" (Fine 1993, 283) abound among ethnographers, researchers never admit to such liaisons. Considering this historical context, Laud's possible omission of sexual detail would not be completely unexpected.

Showing his support for this research, Irving Louis Horowitz, another of Laud's Washington University Ph.D. committee members, published two subsequent articles by Laud in *Trans-action* (1970b, 1971a), including a featured cover-page article in 1970. Laud begins this essay with the emphasis that all social classes are involved in tearooms. And while the race of tearoom participants is also occasionally mentioned in the book, it apparently played no role in preference for sexual partners. In chapter 1 Laud also noted that those frequenting tearooms included working-class men such as uniformed gas station attendants, salesmen, and physicians, and "there exists a sort of democracy that is endemic to impersonal sex. Men of all racial, social, educational, and physical characteristics meet in these places for sexual union" (Humphreys 1970a, 13). The lack of class and racial division in the tearooms illustrates the well-known sociological axiom that to the degree that members of a group feel rejected by all others the social solidarity of the group will increase.

Chapter 2 also deals with the fact that in most ethnographic work no preexisting hypotheses exist. The reasoning in this type of research is inductive rather than deductive, looking for patterns that emerge from one's data. Here Humphreys described his *covert sample selection:* "Following Rainwater's suggestion, I gathered a sample of the tearoom participants by tracing the license plates of the autos they drove to the parks" (Humphreys 1970a, 30). "In September of 1966, then, I set about to gather a sample in as systematic a manner as possible under the circumstances. . . . I took the license plate numbers of as many cars as equaled approximately 10 percent of the average volume," locating drivers' addresses from "friendly policemen" (31, 38). He then interviewed tearoom participants at their homes and told them they were part of a larger sample. "No names or other identifying tags were allowed to appear on the questionnaires. Although I recognized each of the men interviewed from observation in the tearooms, there was no indication that they remembered me. I was careful to change my appearance, dress, and automobile" (42). "My master list was kept in a safe-deposit box. Each interview card, kept under lock and key, was destroyed with completion of the schedule" (42). The worst that can be said about this methodology is that it is possible that some of those interviewed did recognize him and were terrified that he would expose their sexual activities. In this same chapter Humphreys refers to twelve respondents he identified as his "intensive dozen" (36), whom he interviewed at great length. In some of these cases he taped the participants' interviews.

Humphreys's chapter 3 deals with the *role flexibility* that occurs during initial sexual negotiations and *role instability* that results from the aging process. Indeed, in this setting there is a close relationship between *age stratification and sex acts*. Humphreys found that "analyzing the estimated ages of the principal partners in 53 observed acts of fellatio, I arrived at these conclusions: the insertee was judged to be older than the insertor in forty cases; they were approximately the same age in three; and the insertor was the older in ten instances" (Humphreys 1970a, 108). "Nearly always in the observation records, when a man took the insertor role he left for his car immediately after cleansing. The insertee may leave, too, but frequently waits in the tearoom for someone else to enter. Sometimes he becomes the insertor in a subsequent encounter" (76). If age assumes great significance, as it does in heterosexual relationships, social class plays no obvious role in these interaction patterns, and so, in this sense, the tearooms comprise a classless society.

In chapter 4 Humphreys considers the *specific sex acts* that occur in tearooms. Humphreys (1970a, 75) noted, "I have [only] twice seen couples engaging in anal intercourse. This is a form of sexual activity rare in most tearooms, probably due to the greater amount of time required and the drastic rearrangement of clothing involved, both of which tend to increase the danger of being apprehended in the act. Manual masturbation is an occasional means of reaching orgasm, particularly by the urinals or elsewhere in a crowded room." "Manipulation of the other's organ is reciprocated in about half of the cases" (66).

Absent evidence of sexual intercourse, Humphreys notes that the risk of venereal disease is slight. If disease is not a problem, chapter 5 indicates that police decoys and blackmail remain serious problems. Chapter 4 also shows that there were patterns of approaching, positioning, signaling, and contracting, all without words being exchanged. The participants gave consent to fellatio by showing an erection, and thus there was no seduction, violence, or coercion. Laud noted "the silence of the interaction. . . . Of fifty encounters on which I made extensive notes, only fifteen included vocal utterances" (Humphreys 1970a, 12). Silence was used to maintain the anonymous quality of the relationships as well as for the participants to be alert to possible intrusions.

In the introduction Rainwater also noted that existing law enforcement practices were impossible to justify (Humphreys 1970a, xv): "Humphreys demonstrates that tearooms represent neither the moral danger to unsuspecting youth nor the simple public nuisances of which they have been accused. . . . There is none of the aggressiveness and flaunting of homosexual behavior on which the moral entrepreneurs who encourage and apologize for police crackdowns rely in their support for such crusades." In other words, by dispelling stereotypes about who uses tearooms and how they use them, Laud's research contributes to a more sympathetic understanding of tearoom users. As such, he makes important contributions to the protection of consensual homosexual sex.

In chapter 5 Laud looks at the risks involved in the tearoom trade encounters. These risks include entrapment and arrest by the police, being beaten by teenage toughs, and being discovered by acquaintances. Since physical overtures appear to be made only when the subject of the advance had authorized consent by showing an erect penis, Humphreys questions the police use of decoys who "violate the role of the straight" (Humphreys 1970a, 87) by loitering and attempting to entrap tearoom participants. And "most blackmailing is done by law enforcement personnel as a result of decoy operations" (89). Laud also describes an incident where he was arrested during the course of his research for merely hanging around a restroom.

Chapter 6 describes the various types of tearoom participants and is stereotype-busting in showing that many tearoom participants are conservative heterosexually married men. The largest percentage of Laud's respondents was "trade" (heterosexually married or divorced working-class men such as truck drivers and machine operators). There were also married participants from higher-status occupations to whom Humphreys refers as "ambisexuals." Whereas those in the "trade" category seek out tearooms for furtive sexual relief, "ambisexuals" seek them out for adventure and excitement (Humphreys 1970a, 120). There are also openly gay, unmarried men and "closet queens," but Laud's real contribution is in showing how few of these latter categories there are in contrast to the former. And Laud's findings affirm that "many people with bisexual feelings and experiences choose not to identify themselves as bisexual" (Rust 1996, 134). Perhaps because "all people are clearly either biologically female or male, . . . then all sexual relationships are clearly [assumed to be] between same-sexed/gendered or other-sexed/gendered people and hence either homosexual or heterosexual" (Rodrìguez Rust 2000, 6).

In chapter 6 Humphreys also deals with *political preference and public sex* and notes that "the majority (54 per cent) of my research subjects are married and living with their wives. . . . [Survey data show that they go to great lengths to maintain] exemplary marriages" (Humphreys 1970a, 105). Tearooms "attract a variety of men, a *minority* of whom are active in the homosexual subculture. . . . A large group of them have no homosexual self-identity" (11). There were few self-described liberals in the sample, and most individuals had a "breastplate of righteousness" (137), giving all outward appearances of being model citizens.

Laud further develops the concept of the "breastplate of righteousness" in chapter 7. He argues that the covert deviant wears a "protective shield of superpropriety" (Humphreys 1970a, 135). "Motivated largely by his own awareness of the discreditable nature of his secret behavior, the covert deviant develops a presentation of self that is respectable to a fault. His whole lifestyle becomes an incarnation of what is proper and orthodox. In manners and taste, religion and art, he strives to compensate for an otherwise low resistance to the shock of exposure" (135–36).

For the most part, the men frequenting the tearooms were "afraid of being liberal" and their "social conservatism is revealed as a product of the illegal roles these men play in the hidden moments of their lives" (Humphreys 1970a, 139). As it happens, Laud's own life in the priesthood, his marriage to a beautiful woman, and his rearing of two children reflect elements of the breastplate of righteousness. This is even truer of Laud's father's life. We also see in chapter 5 that the breastplate of righteousness was the focus of Laud's last, and uncompleted, book.

In several parts of *Tearoom Trade,* Humphreys continues the discussion of the design of his survey sample of tearoom participants whom he covertly identified, allowing him to interview them later in their homes. "Once these [initial] interviews were completed, preparations could be made for the final step of the research design. From names appearing in the randomly selected sample of the over-all social health survey, fifty men were selected, matched with the completed questionnaires on the following four characteristics: . . . occupational category, race, area of the metropolitan region . . . and marital status" (Humphreys 1970a, 43). "These last fifty interviews, then, enabled me to compare characteristics of the two samples—one deviant, one control—matched on the basis of certain socioeconomic characteristics, race, and marital status" (43). The control group was clearly less conservative. Illustrative of this conservatism is that the majority of those at the tearooms with out-of-state plates had "stickers that identified the owners as armed forces personnel from nearby military installations" (39). Elsewhere Laud identifies military posts as "other major outlets for homosexual activity" (4). He found that military personnel were more likely to be involved in homosexual activity than were those in the control group. By combining his observational and interview data Laud also found that "all of the ex-Navy men in the deviant sample were observed in the insertee role, whereas the ex-Marines were all insertors" (150).

Humphreys (1970a, 171) considers his research strategy as follows: "I interviewed persons I had observed in the tearooms under the pretext of a social health survey. . . . Is it unethical to use data that someone has gathered for other purposes, one of which is unknown to the respondent? With the employment of proper security precautions, I think such multiple use is quite ethical; it is frequently employed by anyone using such data banks as the records of the Bureau of Census." The question is, "which methods may result in more or less misrepresentation of purposes and identity, more or less betrayal of confidence, and more or less positive or negative consequences for the subjects. The ethics of social science are situation ethics" (170). This assertion was not fully and carefully reasoned, and undoubtedly served as a lightning rod for criticism.

According to Laud, the public record of arrests indicates that there are many right-wing, "moral majority" types who frequent tearooms. He was quoted as saying: "You see, tearoom habitués have a sex-love rift. Because their sexual and affectional lives are not together, they often project their self-hatred onto others. . . . Ironically, some even become moral crusaders, encouraging more vice squad activity and thus contributing to their own oppression" (Miller 1982, 40). Openly gay men feel greater freedom in being openly liberal. In any case, political conservatives could be expected to reject the notion that tearoom participants swell their ranks. Chapter 8 deals with the kicks some men find in public sex, in sexual relations such as these without commitment, and a defense of public sex such as in automobiles and restrooms.

In *Trans-action* Humphreys (1971a) discusses "New Styles in Homosexual Manliness": "By virilization, I refer to the increasingly masculine image of the gay scene. . . . The new emphasis in the homosexual subculture, then, is upon virility: not the hypermasculinity of Muscle Beach and the motorcycle set, for these are part of the old gay world's parody on heterosexuality" (41). "My data indicate that Roman Catholic religious affiliation is a causal factor in tearoom participation, because that church's prohibition of the use of artificial contraceptives limits the sexual outlet in marriage" (41). Having already antagonized the military, this analysis could be expected to outrage many Roman Catholics. Even at this early stage in his academic career, Laud felt no need to adhere to any norms of scholarly moderation.

4

Published Criticism and Use of *Tearoom Trade*

The initial reviews were typically neither enthusiastic nor outraged. In the *American Sociological Review* Ira Reiss (1971, 581) noted: "My overall reaction to this book is rather mixed. . . . This unintended use of a public facility is itself a valuable contribution to the study of the urban scene" [and involves] "men of all social classes." The problem is that the book relies far too much on the "use of jargon" (582). A reviewer in the *American Anthropologist* was also lukewarm: "Overall, the treatment of the patrons seems somewhat superficial. One would prefer more depth, greater understanding, and more insight" (Eiselein 1971, 860). This is a curious criticism because insight and understanding are typically considered the primary strengths of the book. The reviewer for the *Library Journal* had additional reservations: "His study raises the question of whether or not it could have broader and more authoritative application had it been conducted by a team which included medicolegal experts" (Sprow 1970, 2704), presumably meaning that lawyers and doctors should have made the tearoom observations. A reviewer for *Contemporary Psychology* (Wiens 1971) merely describes the content of the book, without hazarding any evaluation, noting only that the research was thorough with the participant-observation stage of the data collection lasting approximately two years.

A bit more positive, a reviewer for the *Annals* observes: "From a purely aesthetic point of view, the impersonal, uncommitted homosexual contact is a very dreary and dingy sexual outlet. In terms of this aesthetic dimension, I admire Humphreys's tenacity in pursuing this project to its conclusion" (Lavin 1971, 200). A review in the *Archives of*

Sexual Behavior calls this book "a remarkable achievement" (Hoffman 1971, 98) [for] "Humphreys's book does cause us all to confront some of our prejudices, and for that, among the many other things it gives us, we must be grateful" (100). "While all proper liberals now agree that consensual sex in private should not be subject to the criminal law, what about consensual sex *in public?*" (100). The consulting editor of the *Criminal Law Bulletin* (Cohen 1971, 67) gave the most positive review: "It is a most unusual book about men who, despite our preconceptions, turn out to be not so unusual. . . . Much of our knowledge about sexual behavior in general comes from interviews, clinical case histories, gamey courtroom stories, and locker room anecdotes. Here, for the first time, a participant-observer tells it like it is instead of how others say it is." Still, Cohen raises an issue: "Does a man who engages in criminal conduct . . . in a public facility, in effect waive his rights to privacy and dignity?" (68). Considering that most arrests for consensual homosexual activities involve activities in public restrooms, perhaps some rethinking of the definition of private and public is required. "Humphreys' work has the effect of raising profound questions as to what is private. If 'in private' is simply another aspect of consent—consent to be approached, to view and to engage . . . the games people play in tearooms may be no less private than those played at cocktail parties" (69), and thus law enforcement should cease its surveillance of restrooms in search of sexual encounters.

Soon after the publication of *Tearoom Trade* in 1970 Laud and his publisher, Aldine, recognized the explosive impact of the book on debates concerning the ethics of covert social science research. Thus in the second edition, published in 1975, some of the most stinging criticisms were included in a new concluding section entitled "Retrospect: Ethical Issues in Social Research." Samples of these critiques are reproduced in the paragraphs below.

Syndicated columnist Nicholas von Hoffman turned this research into a nationally visible issue. Von Hoffman argued that, although Humphreys believed in his own good motives, good motives were not sufficient, since "J. Edgar Hoover unquestionably believes he's protecting the country against subversion when he orders your telephone tapped" (von Hoffman 1975, 179). In this same vein von Hoffman also mentions that Richard Nixon's attorney general, John Mitchell, and his Justice Department could justify any of their tactics, using guilt by association to condemn Laud. Von Hoffman also argued that, "incontestably such information is useful to parents, to teen-agers themselves, to policemen, legislators and many others, but it is done by invading some people's privacy. My newspaper could probably learn a lot of things that the public has a right and need to know if its reporters were to use disguises and the gimmickry of modern, transistorized, domestic espionage, but there is a policy against it. No information is valuable enough to obtain by nipping away at personal liberty, and this is true no matter who's doing the gnawing" (181).

Myron Glazer was more calculating and moderate in his ethical assessment of Laud's research. While questioning the later survey of tearoom participants, Glazer notes that "his first encounter with men occurred in a *public* bathroom. He had as much right to be there as any of the participants. Indeed, as the lookout, he took the same risks as those he observed. Arrest, harassment, and physical violence could have been his lot" (Glazer 1975, 216-17). Another observer has noted that this phase of the study can be seen as involving a voluntary exchange of services (Dworkin 1982).

The most damaging criticism came from within the ranks of the academic community. Laud (1975, 225) noted that sociologist Barry Krisberg in the left-leaning journal *Issues in Criminology* condemned *Tearoom Trade*, as well as Becker's research on marihuana users and dance band musicians, Liebow's study of homeless black men, Polsky's research on poolroom hustlers, and Goffman's classic study of patients in psychiatric hospitals. Sociologist Donald Warwick notes that Humphreys deceived the police to get access to auto license numbers. Deceiving the police seems especially appalling to Warwick. Warwick was so outraged by this deception that he engages in gross hyperbole in comparing Laud's research to that of "medical experimentation carried out in Nazi Germany" (1975a, 202). And this research is so repugnant to Warwick that there is plenty of blame to spread around. "In a larger sense, both Humphreys and the project director of the 'social health survey' may have distorted that study by allowing a sub-sample of 50 homosexuals to be blended into the total cross-section" (201).

According to Warwick, four parties are involved in research involving human subjects: subjects, the researcher, the researcher's profession, and the entire host society. "Recent experience with field interviewing suggests that this 'public be damned' attitude is producing a growing backlash against social research" (Warwick 1975a, 208). "If Humphreys' study contributes to public suspicion about the trustworthiness of social scientists, as I think it does, then my freedom and that of my professional colleagues to do our kinds of research will suffer accordingly" (197).

So this is really the nub of the issue. The possible loss of status for the discipline is primarily how Warwick's analysis of the problem is framed. For Warwick, professional freedom is similar to a cake. You only have it if you do not attempt to use it. In any case, Warwick concluded in *Psychology Today* (1975b, 105) that, although Laud argued that he was assisting the gay community with his research, "I cannot believe that such data will really improve the lot of homosexuals. Even if it did, Humphreys' chain of lies was not morally justified." Laud retorted: "Our concern about possible research consequences for our fellow 'professionals' should take a secondary place to concern for those who may benefit from our research" (Humphreys 1975, 169).

Perhaps much of the outrage occasioned by *Tearoom Trade* was a consequence of the nature of the subjects used here. Previous fieldwork had focused on working class, minority, and publicly deviant subjects. On the other hand, Laud's research included men from all social classes, including a good representation of the conservative middle classes, shown to be less virtuous than they claimed. It seems to have been more generally acceptable to study the behavior of working-class males (Whyte 1955), including the same-sex activities of the lower-class juveniles (Reiss 1961), the sexual exploits of homeless black men (Liebow 1967), the activities of jazz musicians (Becker 1963), and pool hustlers (Polsky 1967).

Coincidentally, in 1969 sociologist-field-worker Ned Polsky was chair of the Society for the Study of Social Problems (SSSP), C. Wright Mills Book Award Committee, and reported, in 1970, that *Tearoom Trade* had received the 1969 C. Wright Mills Award. Here it was noted: "This award is intended to recognize outstanding research and writing on critical social issues in the tradition of the late C. Wright Mills." In response to the book receiving this award, Alvin Gouldner took another swipe (this one in print) at his old enemy: "And look what we get: papers on 'Watch Queens' and homosexuals diddling one another in public toilets! When we gave the C. Wright Mills award for that trivia, one had to begin to suspect that it was all over for the Society [the SSSP]. And it probably is" (Gouldner 1976, 41). Nearly three decades later, as we enter the new millennium, it is clear that these prophecies of the death of the SSSP were greatly exaggerated.

A Defense Is Mounted

The book was favorably reviewed in England. Cowan (1970) argued that "this book illuminates a dark corner of sexual life. . . . As such it is a valid contribution." Another reviewer in the United Kingdom contends that Laud, "cuts through any sniggering in a few pages. He immediately convinces the reader that he is engaged in a serious moral and sociological enterprise. . . . His prose is honest, cool, perfectly consistent in its use of everyday terms . . . and involves a most ingenious piece of sampling methodology. . . . His policy recommendations are sensible and humane" (Taylor 1970).

Humphreys asked: "Are there, perhaps, some areas of human behavior that are not fit for social scientific study at all? Should sex, religion, suicide or other socially sensitive concerns be omitted from the catalogue of possible fields of sociological research? Some say 'let sleeping dogs lie'" (Humphreys 1975, 167–68). "We are not, however, protecting a harassed population of deviants by refusing to look at them" (169), for this allows stereotypes to persist.

In an exchange with von Hoffman originally published in *Trans-Action* magazine in 1970, Horowitz and Lee Rainwater argued that politicians, clergy, and the press were on the attack: "And so, these past few years, sociologists have been getting their lumps from these various groups" (Horowitz and Rainwater 1975, 182). This is "an issue that has grown almost imperceptibly over the last few years, and now [it] threatens to create in the next decade a tame sociology to replace the fairly robust one that developed during the sixties" (181). Yet "ethnographic research is a powerful tool for social understanding and policy making" (190).

Horowitz and Rainwater (1975, 189) frame the issue in these terms: "the right to privacy of the researcher over and against the wishes of established authority." "Sociologists uphold the right to know in a context of the surest protection for the integrity of the subject matter and the private rights of the people studied" (185). In any event, as a practical matter they concluded the following about Laud's methodology: "Had he not conducted the follow-up interviews, we would once again be thrown back on simple-minded, psychological explanations that are truly more voyeuristic than analytic" (187). Humphreys could not have told respondents in the survey the truth since this would have been devastating for them. Whereas Warwick wants professional status, Horowitz and Rainwater emphasize professional freedom.

In the rush to criticize the research methodology, data from the book are often overlooked (Nardi 1995). The behavior observed shows no violence, no coercion, no involvement of youths, and almost no anal intercourse, reducing the threat of sexually transmitted diseases. The subsequent survey data show participants to be normal to a fault. There are no drag queens found here, no radical politics, but, instead, primarily model, conservative citizens.

On Balance: Real and Imagined Consequences

Anthropologist Joan Cassell was not impressed with Humphreys's research. Although she agreed that it "apparently caused no harm," "knowing just what goes on in brief homosexual encounters in public restrooms, . . . is no more vital than much of the material in the *National Inquirer"* (1982, 18). Thus, in her view, there is no good reason to support this line of research even if it caused no harm given that its salacious content made it little more than pornography.

Prominent feminist sociologist Arlene Kaplan Daniels rejected the methodology of *Tearoom Trade,* reasoning that even psychiatrists often disclose the identities of their patients (Glazer 1975, 219). According to her reasoning, if even psychiatrists misbehave, sociologists should be circumscribed to prevent similar abuses. She argued: "I have very grave doubts about the argument that we should rely upon Humphreys' personal sense of honor, ethics, or professional discretion, no matter how well developed these traits are in him." Consistent with Daniels's concerns, Nicholas von Hoffman argued that information collected could have been used for blackmail, but it wasn't. The information could have been distributed to an undergraduate class, but it wasn't. It could have been distributed to friends at a party, but it wasn't.

The misuse of personal information collected in the course of professional practice is possible for many professions, including law, the clergy, and medicine. Humphreys clearly recognized this possibility and he wrote that, "after my research became a public controversy to protect human subjects I spent some weeks early in the summer of 1968 burning tapes, deleting passages from transcripts, and feeding material into a shredder" (1975, 229). Accordingly, Glazer wrote (1975, 200): "My conversations with Humphreys convinced me of his extraordinary courage and ability to withstand condemnation and abuse. Yet these very characteristics make him a poor model for others to emulate without the most painful self-scrutiny." While Glazer is quite correct in emphasizing Humphreys's special courage, this makes Humphreys an especially good role model in our view. Yet Glazer cautions (1975, 200): "Had Humphreys faltered, had his data been secured by police officials or unscrupulous blackmailers, Humphreys would have been branded a rogue and a fool." But he did not falter, even though he was widely branded as a rogue.

It is true that Humphreys assumed a major professional responsibility that sociologists should take on only after sober reflection. Just how sober was his reflection is demonstrated by the fact that Laud allowed himself to be arrested one afternoon when standing near a tearoom, rather than reveal that he was there to conduct research. He was taken into custody, transported to the police station, questioned, frisked, locked in a cell, and charged with loitering. As Humphreys recalled, "Because I am a minister and have an astute attorney, my case never appeared in court. I am an arrest statistic, not a conviction statistic. [Other men without legal resources] could have been ruined" (1970a, 96). Their families and careers could have been destroyed for the mere act of standing near a tearoom. Violence was also a risk in this research. On one occasion a group of up to sixteen teenage "toughs" surrounded Humphreys and others in a tearoom. After those inside had barricaded the door, the young men unleashed "a barrage of stones and bottles which broke every window in the facility" (Humphreys 1970a, 99).

Myron Glazer (1975, 214) noted (as mentioned above): "soon after completion of his dissertation, officials at Washington University at St. Louis began to raise serious questions about the methodology. Charges were leveled that the disguised observations violated the stipulations of Humphreys' grant from the National Institute of Mental Health regarding the protection of subjects. The Chancellor of the university informed the NIMH of these concerns and asked that another grant largely earmarked for Lee Rainwater, Humphreys' advisor, be held up pending an investigation." Humphreys (1975, 228) also recalled that, "the Chancellor of Washington University argued that I had committed numerous felonies in the course of my research [by aiding and abetting criminal sex acts]. He was not successful in having my degree revoked on this basis, but he did terminate my teaching contract and my participation in a research grant."

Tearoom Trade in Retrospect
The Limitations of Counting Citations

Clawson and Zussman (1998) noted that the *Social Science Citation Index* (SSCI) produces a list of sources that are used by those who write articles. On the other hand, few of those who publish highly influential books have ever published an article in the *American Journal of Sociology* or the *American Sociological Review*. Thus there is "evidence of the enormity of the distance between sociology's book culture and its article culture" (8). To a considerable extent articles tend to cite other articles, and books tend to cite other books. With this in mind, rather than use a simple citation count from the SSCI to determine the significance of *Tearoom Trade*, we will turn to its use in introductory sociology textbooks and social science methods texts, its use by ethnographers, as well as its significance for emerging "queer theory."

Tearoom Trade *in Sociology Textbooks: The Good, the Bad, and the Ugly*

Introductory sociology textbooks were reviewed for the manner in which they presented Laud's research to the beginning college student. Such textbooks were identified from two sources: introductory textbooks available in the University of Missouri library and review copies of textbooks for introduction to sociology supplied by six leading publishers.

Among the books in our library sample, Hess and her coauthors in their introductory text take Humphreys to task for a myriad of alleged ethical lapses including warning others of the approach of law enforcement authorities: "in serving as a lookout to warn the participants of approaching police, Humphreys engaged in illegal behavior" (Hess, Markson, and Stein 1985, 49). It is well to keep in mind that the crimes involved were sodomy and having sexual relations in a public place. Describing it as unethical to assist these men in avoiding arrest seems itself to represent a moral vacuum, namely, allowing the state to determine what is both illegal and unethical. Hess et al. also claim that Humphreys was guilty of "following innocent subjects to their homes, conducting interviews under less than fully honest circumstances and publishing the findings without the consent of the observed" (49). One should note the internal inconsistency in this critique. Initially law violators are evading law enforcement, but almost immediately thereafter they are considered "innocent subjects." Finally, it is implied that Humphreys actually trailed subjects to their homes from the tearooms, and this, of course, is incorrect.

Kornblum's introductory text also implies immediate, hot pursuit: "But [Humphreys] also followed some of the men home and conducted interviews with them there" (Kornblum 2000, 45). On this basis Kornblum suggests that Humphreys's study was largely responsible for the creation of University Institutional Review Boards (IRBs), a development Kornblum applauds. There is no doubt that *Tearoom Trade* did play a significant role in the creation of IRBs. There is, or should be, some debate about whether this has been a positive factor for sociology or for society as a whole (Hessler and Galliher 1983).

To acquire a sense of the textbooks available in May 2001 we contacted six major publishers for review copies of introductory textbooks. This survey uncovered the following discussions of *Tearoom Trade:*

Citing organizational authority, Popenoe (2000, 49) notes that official statements on research ethics "recognize that social research is a two-way process. Potential subjects should know what the research is about; they should also find out what benefits they may gain from it." In another text Shepard (2002) assumes the Code of Ethics of the American Sociological Association (ASA) to be the supreme arbiter of professional morality. (In the last chapter we question this assertion.) In any event, Shepard asks and answers the question in this way: "Did Humphreys violate the [ASA] code of ethics as a covert participant observer? Yes, Humphreys violated the privacy of these people. Most did not want their sexual activities known, and Humphreys did not give them the opportunity to refuse to participate in the study. Humphreys also deceived the men by misrepresenting himself in both the tearooms and their homes. Finally, by recording his observations, Humphreys placed these people in jeopardy of public exposure, arrest, or loss of employment" (Shepard 2002, 56). To his credit, Shepard acknowledges that, "actually, because of his precautions, none of the subjects was injured as a result of his research. In fact, to protect their identities, Humphreys even allowed himself to be arrested" (56). In addition to these questions, Thompson and Hickey (1999, 48) imply that Humphreys's motive for not disclosing his identity as a researcher was the fear of physical reprisal: "Having already been jailed, locked in a restroom, and attacked by a group of teenage 'gay bashers,' Humphreys did not wish to risk physical harm at the hands of his subjects."

Sullivan (2001, 31) sees the ethical issues in these terms: "Even though the men were clearly trying to hide their behavior from prying eyes, Humphreys made his observations without seeking their approval. . . . Issues of privacy, confidentiality, and informed consent are especially important in Humphreys' research because the men observed were engaging in highly stigmatized behavior. If the behavior became public knowledge, it might have changed their lives, since many of the men were married and had children."

Lindsey and Beach (2002, 55–56) agree that, "although subject confidentiality was maintained, these men were no longer anonymous once

Humphreys had their names. Their lives could literally have been ruined if their identities had been divulged." Some textbooks use Humphreys himself as a source of approbation. Henslin (2001a, 144) notes that Humphreys first defended his covert research role, "but five years later, in a second edition of his book (1975), he stated that he should have identified himself as a researcher." Scott and Schwartz (2000) also note Laud's change of heart in the second edition of *Tearoom Trade,* as does Robertson (1987). What Henslin, Scott, Robertson, and Schwartz do not say, however, is that Humphreys admitted a change in heart only regarding the use of license plate numbers in determining interview subjects after his fieldwork (Humphreys 1975, 230), not the fieldwork itself.

In fairness to Henslin, however, unlike the banal distant objectivity of most textbooks, Henslin (2001a, 144) mentions his own involvement in Humphreys's research: "Concerned about protecting the identity of his respondents, Humphreys hid his master list in a safe deposit box. As the controversy grew more heated and a court case loomed, Humphreys feared he might get subpoenaed. He gave me the master list to take from Missouri to Illinois, where I had begun teaching. . . . When he called and asked me to destroy it, I burned it in my backyard." In the final analysis, however, none of the textbooks defend Humphreys's right to do this type of research.

In addition to introductory sociology textbooks, *Tearoom Trade* also comes under scrutiny as an example of "bad ethics" in social science methodology textbooks. While methods texts generally provide a more detailed context for Humphreys's study than do introductory texts, they nonetheless still tend to use it as a negative example. The following illustration from Berg's (1995, 203) *Qualitative Research Methods* is typical: "Another example of research with questionable ethics is Humphreys' (1970) study of casual homosexual encounters, *Tearoom Trade*. . . . While serving as a watch queen (a voyeuristic lookout), Humphreys was able both to observe the encounters and to catch a glimpse of participants' license plates. [With this information, Berg notes, Humphreys located their home addresses and later] deceived these men into thinking he was conducting a survey in their neighborhood. . . . [A]fter the publication of Humphreys' work in 1970, there was a considerable outcry against the invasion of privacy, [and the] misrepresentation of researcher identities, . . . Many of the controversies that revolve around Humphreys' research remain key ethical issues today."

Ultimately, most directly argue, or at least imply, that where *harm* is possible it should weigh more heavily in the decision not to conduct the research than *benefits* should weigh in the decision to proceed with the research. Some authors even raise the issue of whether benefits of any type or magnitude ever justify deception. For instance, Beauchamp et al. (1982, 13) write, "Considered apart from their consequences, deceptive practices such as those Humphreys used appear to many to disrespect [*sic*] the people deceived. . . . These controversies raise basic questions concerning the proper justification of moral conclusions, for they call into question the justificatory relevance of consequentialist considerations. Some believe, for instance, that the moral wrong entailed by deception is of a sort that cannot be justified by appeals to beneficial consequences of any magnitude." While Beauchamp et al. open the possibility of other forms of ethical debate, utilitarian analysis is still the predominant way that methods textbooks evaluate *Tearoom Trade*. This being true we will also use such a framework to understand the ethical implications of this research. It is essential to consider *possible benefits* of this investigation, *possible risks,* and *demonstrated harms* to individuals and to groups.

Considering benefits, Laud Humphreys argued that men involved in homosexual activity as a group would benefit from these results by correcting "the superstition and cruelty" that traditionally have plagued this group (Humphreys 1970a, 173). There is no evidence of the seduction of the young nor was there any use of violence or the spread of disease. Moreover, that many of the participants were respectable, successful, and conservative married men may help to normalize homosexual behavior in the mind of the general public. While all this is true, it also seems plausible that these results may harm the reputation of the "closet homosexual" by broadcasting his previously private behavioral patterns.

The potential risks to subjects, the researcher, and to others must also be considered. Of course, researchers can assume the legal risks that Laud freely accepted. If researchers can make such an informed choice, the potential legal jeopardy of Laud's subjects is of greater concern (Dooley 1995), even though none were ever prosecuted or publicly embarrassed. Finally, there is the risk to the reputation of moral conservatives as a group, since Laud demonstrates that those in such groups are attracted to tearooms. We will leave the damage to the political Right for others to assess.

The concern of the greatest magnitude, however, refers to the demonstrated harms to groups and individuals. First is the issue of harm to research subjects contacted in the survey at their homes. There is no evidence that any of Laud's subjects recognized him, at least that is what

Laud tells us. There is also a concern about the harm of this research to the reputation of sociology (Cassell 1982). According to Humphreys, a vibrant sociology cares little for its reputation and "concern about 'professional integrity,' it seems to me, is symptomatic of a dying discipline" (1970a, 168). It is true, however, that this research contributed to the constantly shrinking private space in the modern world (Kelman 1982). Hidden cameras and undercover police are increasingly a part of our lives, and Laud's research represents one small additional step in that same direction. Even so, there are few demonstrated harms, and we have learned something about public homosexual behavior that normalizes its participants and dispels potentially harmful and dangerous stereotypes.

The Impact of *Tearoom Trade* on Contemporary Urban Ethnographers

The journal *Urban Life and Culture,* since 1987 entitled the *Journal of Contemporary Ethnography,* published numerous articles citing *Tearoom Trade* that study space, place, and behavior, including sexual behavior. This journal began publication in 1972, just two years after *Tearoom Trade* was published. Given this timing the journal is an ideal source for assessing the impact of *Tearoom Trade* on ethnographic research. It appears from this review that *Tearoom Trade* provided an immediate and significant impetus to innovative types of research.

Sexually Diverse People and Their Places

Corzine and Kirby (1977) reported on a study of males who cruise truck stops for sex with drivers. They noted the nearly total silence in these sexual encounters around truck stops. They based their findings on forty informal conversations and ten interviews with twenty-five cruisers. Most of these encounters occurred between 10:00 P.M. and 5:00 A.M. Some cruisers were gay and some bisexual—called "ambisexual" by Humphreys. Opening questions included asking for the time or for a match. There was always the threat of intrusions in such interactions, but no watchqueen roles were discovered. In fact, if Humphreys's role as a watchqueen is discounted, one wonders if any such activity exists.

In a fashion similar to these cruisers, Shover (1975) found that those buying or selling "tarnished good and services" tend to do so without extended conversation. This is true whether the transaction involves swinging couples, illegal abortions, moonshine, prostitution, or illegal drugs. Some sense of privacy was maintained by limiting utterances. Blumstein and Schwartz (1976) reported on the intricacies of bisexuality in men. They noted that "many men have both the ability, and often the preference for engaging in anonymous or 'impersonal' sex" (341). This included heterosexual behavior among self-identified homosexual men and homosexual behavior among heterosexual men. Some bisexual men felt that their orientation was politically correct in that it clearly avoided the oppression of being anti-homosexual. Yet "among the gay activist elements of the community there is often a political rejection of bisexuality, since failure to assume a homosexual identity is viewed as contrary to gay liberation" (346). It was this rejection that possibly put pressure on Humphreys to come out soon after *Tearoom Trade* was initially published.

Heterosexual Places

Lilly and Ball (1981, 181) reported on a "confidential, no-tell, motel" that catered to heterosexual, one-night stands. The staff at this motel screened out potentially troublesome guests (including those with children and those who announced that they intended to spend the entire night), who were not aware that its clients are those who use it as a heterosexual rendezvous. Such naive tourists were typically told that there were no vacancies. The rooms had garages with electronically controlled doors and provided for payment left in the room. Both these factors eliminated the necessity of customers going to the office. The rooms also were equipped with X-rated movies. For those who did go to the office, eye contact was seldom made, allowing a greater sense of privacy. The local police were well aware of the motel's actual and intended use, and in fact received a special professional rate reduction when they used the motel.

Karp (1973) reported on how men hide in pornographic bookstores around the Times Square area of New York City; even in mass society people routinely attempt to hide "unconventional behaviors from total strangers" (428). "When it comes to maintaining a proper image of ourselves, everyone counts" (434). Some bookstore patrons engaged in "waiting" (437) behavior prior to entering to ensure that their entry was not being observed. Patrons also engaged in "skipping" to other stores in the area with different products prior to entering and immediately after leaving to make it difficult to observe their actual consumer interests. The bookstores also often provided "some kind of shielding" such as painted windows (439), making it difficult to see into the bookstore from outside. Once inside the bookstore the norms for social interaction appeared to "demand silence and careful avoidance of either eye or physical contact" (440). The stores provided wide aisles to avoid any possibility that customers will accidentally brush up against one another. Bookstore employees carefully enforced the norms of social interaction. And when merchandise was being purchased, it was rare for any conversation to occur between the stores' workers and customers. Patrons typically scooped up their change and left the store immediately without even seeing if the amount was correct.

Sundholm (1973) reported on an arcade "peep show," showing pornography on individual machines. The machines were designed to ensure privacy for the viewer. Next to the viewing slot was a large, movable shield that hides the viewer's face while he is watching a movie. On top of the machine was a red light that is lit only when the machine was occupied and in operation. This light presumably also served to protect patrons from intrusions. Patrons usually came alone, often looking up and down the street to make sure no one observed their entry into the arcade. Once in the arcade they often moved directly to a vacant machine without looking around at other patrons. Little or no conversation was exchanged between patrons and the cashier. Customers often merely extended paper currency waiting for the cashier to provide coins that the machines would accept. At times the patrons masturbated in the rear of the arcade.

The maintenance of privacy was also significant in Donnelly's (1981) description of two pornographic movie theaters. Patrons came to the theater alone or as couples or in groups. Those coming to the arcade alone were always men. In the larger theater the single men always sat at the back, the couples in the middle, and groups near the front. The single men always left several seats between themselves and other single patrons, and were often hunched down in their seats to maintain some degree of privacy.

Homosexual People and Places

Mileski and Black (1972, 190–91) observed that homosexual territories "are by no means obvious to the untrained eye." In any event, in most of these territories "direct approaches are taboo" (193) except "in highly specialized settings of an orgiastic sort (such as steambaths)" (193). Approaches were often subtle and involved indirect eye contact. In making such interpersonal contacts "the escalation process is fragile, with the exchange of cues by its nature allowing for a graceful exit by either or both parties at any point" (194).

Lee (1979) reported on the "institutional completeness of the gay community" (179). Gay residents of Toronto can draw on gay real estate agents, gay lawyers, gay insurance agents, gay house cleaning services, gay skilled labor, gay bars, and can even use a Gay Yellow Pages. The gay population of the city tends to be concentrated at the city's core. Gay bars developed after a period of police tolerance of a mixed-use bar. "Gay time" (187) involves evening homosexual use of spaces frequented by heterosexuals during the day. Styles (1979) studied the behavior in gay baths. He gained entry into a private bathhouse by asking a gay friend to vouch for him. Initially he attempted to merely talk with participants, but learned by not involving himself in sex that they ceased being interested in talking. In fact, much of what went on involved nonverbal communication. After becoming involved in sexual encounters in the bathhouse, Styles felt he became much more aware of what was going on there.

As a group these diverse studies show that somehow privacy is maintained even in intimate, very personal settings. Rules of social interaction in locations as diverse as truck stops, toilets, motels, pornographic bookstores, and theaters require communication but limit it in some prescribed manner. By controlling either verbal utterances or eye contact discreditable activity proceeds but with the necessary assurances of confidentiality for all those involved. *Tearoom Trade* made researchers aware of the possibility of such patterns.

Toilets as Largely Unstudied Places

While Hughes, Blumer, and others in the Chicago school sent their students out into the community to study police, funeral directors, physicians, drug addicts, and organized crime, there is no record of these observers studying restroom interactions. Cahill and his colleagues (1985), on the other hand, citing the fieldwork of Humphreys, studied social interaction in both male and female toilets. They noted that to provide some privacy, partially walled cubicles with doors may surround toilets. They also observed that when men who were acquaintances were using adjacent urinals they spoke to each other but did not look at each other to maintain some sense of privacy. Thus communication using words, but not visual contact, provided the necessary distance. Additionally, when an individual has defecated, the others present typically ignored the consequent odor. These patterns illustrate the unwritten rules of social interaction in toilets.

The Influence of Tearoom Trade's *Methods*

Horowitz (1986) described the difficulties in being a woman who was studying a male street gang. She was initially considered to be a "Lady Reporter" (414) but ultimately was considered an "inside-outsider" (423). This is similar to Humphreys's experience. At the time he conducted his research he was supposedly an openly straight man who was studying men who had various public identities, yet all of whom were involved in homosexual sex.

Warren (1980) discussed the effects and ethics of social science research. She distinguished extreme effects on individuals such as loss of a "job or change of lifestyle" (283), compared to "long-term effects on the collectivity" (284). Researchers can also be negatively affected by their own research because of the negative reactions of colleagues or university administrators, citing Humphreys "difficulties with the [Washington University] administration" (301). Other ethical considerations emerge from Plummer's (1999) argument that ethnographies have the capacity to give voice to those who would otherwise be ignored in a society. This was clearly the case for the participants of tearooms through Humphreys's research.

Four studies used *Tearoom Trade* in their list of references apparently to add legitimacy to their articles. Chapoulie (1987) wrote about the fieldwork tradition of Hughes, which Humphreys's work builds on and enhances. Shulman (1994) studied private investigators and their "dirty data and investigative methods" (214). Shulman conducted interviews with twenty private investigators. Private investigators use some of the methods Humphreys employed, including of course, extended observations in public places and the tracing of license plate numbers. Karp (1992) reported on a group of people "suffering from depression or manic depression" (139) who met weekly in a discussion and support group. The group had been in existence for five years and had grown from nearly 50 participants to approximately 120. The group met in a psychiatric hospital. Participants often observed that they were the victims of "faulty brain chemistry" (153). While some of the participants felt that they had located a good psychiatrist, "the more typical pattern appeared to be disillusionment about the efficacy of psychiatry" (160). In the group meetings, discussions often centered on an individual who was beginning to take a new drug and attempted to inform a participant as to what to expect. Thus this is a study of marginalized people in their own place, similar to *Tearoom Trade*. Zimmerman and Wieder (1977) reported on the use of data from a diary that subjects were asked to maintain which then can be used as the basis for interviews. Although Humphreys did not use this technique, he could have done so with the subjects he interviewed in depth.

Tearoom Trade's Contribution to Queer Theory

During the 1990s "queer theory" exploded onto the academic scene. As Chauncey (2000, 302) has observed: "Then, almost overnight, everything changed . . . the late 1980s and early 1990s witnessed a sudden, unprecedented, and extraordinary growth in the field." Rather than avoiding this pejorative term, those writing in this genre embrace the word by redefining its meaning. In the growth of this new usage, however, "queer theory and sociology have barely acknowledged one another. . . . Sociologists have been almost invisible in these discussions" (Seidman 1996, 13). Yet an exchange of ideas could be very valuable, since "queer theory suggests to sociologists a more reflexive analysis of sexual categories and the ways these sexual meanings intersect with institutions to shape dynamics of order and oppression. Sociologists, in turn, have something crucial to offer [by bringing an] empirical richness to the often literary or abstract conceptual analyses of Queer theory" (17). Although this is seldom recognized, we argue that Humphreys's work in *Tearoom Trade* laid the empirical groundwork for some of queer theory's insights into the dynamics and ambiguities of sexual identity by providing just such an empirical richness.

According to Sedgwick (1990), to understand Western society it is essential to critically analyze the distinction between "heterosexuals" and "homosexuals." Another writer observes that "much is invested culturally in representing homosexuality as definitionally unproblematic, and in maintaining heterosexuality and homosexuality as radically and demonstrably distinct from one another" (Jagose 1996, 18). Seidman (1996, 12) refers to this distinction as "categories of knowledge." Similarly Turner (2000) notes that "queer theorists . . . investigate the historical and cultural underpinnings of nouns such as . . . 'homosexual,' 'gay,' and 'lesbian,' in order to examine what sorts of generalizations and assumptions . . . determine the meanings, of those terms." "We ignore unique aspects of . . . queers by referring to them as . . . 'homosexual.'" Some force people into these categories when neither "the categories nor the persons who fit them should exist at all" (33). "Assigning persons to categories . . . depends on relations of authority, power, and force operating in specific institutions. . . . [Q]ueer theorists insist that persons do not divide so neatly into binary categories" such as "heterosexual/homosexual" (34). Thus "queer theory and queer studies propose a focus not so much on specific populations as on sexual categorization processes and their deconstruction" (Gamson 2000, 349).

In contemporary usage homosexuality draws "attention to the paradigm shift from sexual acts to sexual identities" (Jagose 1996, 18). A failure to appreciate this complexity led to an initial misconception of AIDS as a gay disease, only later recognized as a problem for the "general population" (20). The importance of separating homosexual identity and same-sex behavior is clear from the difficulty in attempting health education for "men who have sex with other men but do not identify themselves as gay" (20). "Central to Queer theory [is] its challenge to . . . the assumption of a unified homosexual identity. . . . Queer theorists argue that identities are always multiple" (Seidman 1996, 11). Bisexuality became a much more central subject in queer studies for its "capacity to confound sex and gender categories" (Gamson 2000, 355).

This complexity is precisely what Humphreys illustrated in his tearoom research and even in his own life. The men whose private behavior he observed in the tearooms included all variety of sexual and political orientations in their public lives. Although a few publicly identified themselves as gay, most identified themselves and lived their daily lives as heterosexuals, only "commuting" to homosexuality for relatively brief periods (see also Brekhus 2003, 48–73). In Humphreys's own public life he was initially heterosexual, then bisexual, an admitted participant in tearoom sex, and, finally, publicly gay. Whatever other contributions of *Tearoom Trade*, in the final analysis it should be noted that recently the response to this work has become more varied and more positive, and, in any event, the book is still in print more than thirty years after its original publication.

Laud Humphreys, 1940s (courtesy of Clair Humphreys Beller)

Laud Humphreys, 1950s (courtesy of Clair Humphreys Beller)

Nancy and Laud Humphreys, 1960 (courtesy of Clair Humphreys Beller)

Right: Nancy Humphreys with Clair and David Humphreys, 1960s (courtesy of Clair Humphreys Beller)

Below: David, Clair, Nancy, and Laud Humphreys, circa 1970 (courtesy of Clair Humphreys Beller)

Laud Humphreys, circa 1969 (courtesy of Clair Humphreys Beller)

Interior of restroom, Forest Park, St. Louis, Missouri

Exterior of restroom, Forest Park, St. Louis, Missouri

Brian Miller, 1970s (courtesy of Brian Miller)

Laud Humphreys, 1970s (courtesy of Clair Humphreys Beller)

Laud Humphreys, 1980s (courtesy of Clair Humphreys Beller)

Laud Humphreys, 1980s (courtesy of Clair Humphreys Beller)

5

Upward Professional Mobility and Continuing Activism

Civil Disobedience in Southern Illinois

Immediately after receiving his Ph.D. in 1968 Laud Humphreys accepted a position as assistant professor at Southern Illinois University (SIU) at Edwardsville. He remained in this position until 1970. James Henslin, his fellow graduate student at Washington University, finished his degree just prior to Laud and accepted a position at SIU. When another opening in sociology became available he recommended Laud for the position (Henslin 2001b). Prior to Gouldner's assault on Humphreys, Henslin recalled that Laud was to have been employed as an assistant professor at Washington University (Henslin 2001a). Rainwater (2001) explained, "I had a large grant which Laud was going to work on." After the Gouldner incident, the arrangement was called off. Undoubtedly the university felt it would be better to keep the two as far apart as possible. Humphreys's controversial research was also a central issue (Henslin 2001a).

At SIU Humphreys was ever vigilant as a social and political activist. In September 1968, soon after arriving at SIU, he wrote to the president of the Midwest Sociological Society asking that the organization cancel their Chicago meetings (Humphreys 1968a). He explained that this would provide a symbolic protest to the brutal police repression of the demonstrators at the Democratic National Convention earlier that year.

While Humphreys was at SIU he predictably got into trouble. At one point the father of a male student sent a letter to the administration complaining that Laud was attempting to seduce his son (Henslin 2001b). The letter eventually found its way to the chancellor's office. Since Laud was married, the chancellor did not take it seriously and merely sent Laud a copy of the letter. In August 1969 Laud was involved in a confrontation with a university police officer. The officer had asked him to move his car from a service road to a parking lot. According to a written police report, in response to this demand Laud had replied: "Fuck the Chancellor" (SIU Police 1969). When the chancellor sent him a note about this, Laud responded by letter (Humphreys 1969): "Should you wish to discuss this matter further with me, I'd be happy to do so. Otherwise, I shall merely store it away with my other memories of bad experiences with the uniformed representatives of law and order."

Later, near the end of his second and final year at SIU, more serious problems emerged for Humphreys. In May 1970 the SIU campus was the site of student demonstrations, as were many campuses across the nation. According to Henslin, who was one of the leaders of these events, the SIU demonstrations and antiwar speeches were totally non-violent. After these campus activities, Henslin recalled that he went back to his office, and Laud decided to lead a group of students into the town. As they marched, Laud led them in a chant: "'One, Two, Three, Four, we don't want your fucking war.' Laud led a group into the local draft board office. Once inside, Laud climbed onto the counter. . . . Laud took the draft board's mandatory photo of the president off the wall, broke it over his knee, ripped the photo of Nixon apart, and gave it to the demonstrators [in a parody of the Eucharist], saying 'Take and eat.' He then led the group out and they continued to march" (Henslin 2001c).

Clair recalled that soon the family began to receive telephoned death threats, as well as threats to kidnap her and her brother and to burn down the family's house. In fact, flares the sheriff's department used for the stated purpose of increasing visibility around the Humphreys house nearly caused the house to catch fire. The pressure became so intimidating that, toward the end of the third quarter of Laud's second year at SIU, the family had to leave town. The Black Panthers helped to spirit the family safely out of town. Laud noted (1972b, 46) that "my family and I were driven from our home by a mob that had been transported in vehicles owned by the sheriff's department and driven by deputies. . . . Vigilantes had phoned at regular intervals to warn me in advance that they were coming, even specifying the brand of gasoline they were bringing to burn my home." The university president agreed that the situation was so dangerous for Laud and his family that Laud was given permission to leave town before the quarter ended, and his students were allowed to complete their work by mail (Henslin 2001b).

The FBI File on Laud Humphreys

Humphreys's FBI file (see Appendix B) verifies the recollections of his friends and colleagues, and also provides additional details that would otherwise have been lost after three decades. Many FBI files released under the Freedom of Information Act are censored to the point of making them useless as a source of information, and often the FBI delays release of information for years, also minimizing the usefulness of the documents. Journalist Max Frankel (*New York Times Magazine* 2000) reports precisely this experience in receiving his own file. He waited many years to see it, and when it was finally sent to him its contents were almost totally blacked out. This was also our experience in attempting to gain the release of the late Alfred Lindesmith's file (Keys and Galliher 2000). The process took nearly five years and resulted in the release of pages that were over 95 percent excised.

On the other hand, Laud Humphreys's file was sent approximately four months after the initial request, and seems complete save for the deletion of the names of informants throughout the document's sixty-five pages. If the deletions are not a source of great surprise or concern, the first entry in Laud's file is nonetheless ominous. A letter in the file dated February 2, 1966, explains that Laud had issued a formal complaint to the Justice Department about a restaurant in Memphis, Tennessee, where a mixed-race group of which he was a part was denied service. Laud's justifiable complaint was turned back on him and became a permanent part of his own FBI file.

His file also reports that on May 5, 1970, he "destroyed a document and a photograph, which were government property; also disrupted activities of the [draft] board and chanted obscene slogans. [He] led a group of approximately 100 persons. . . . Humphreys jumped up on a desk in the draft board, read a memorandum, which was government property. His reading in part was as follows: 'Emergency action is necessary to insure that the May Induction Call for Illinois is met in full. . . . If an increase in your call is necessary, order the registrant for induction and advise this Headquarters.' . . . After Humphreys read the memorandum, he tore it in quarters and threw it on the floor. . . . Humphreys thereafter ripped a photograph of President Richard M. Nixon from the wall of the draft board, smashing it on a desk, breaking the glass and thereafter tore the picture from the frame and tore the picture into several pieces. . . . The group entered through a door marked 'no admittance,' which door was waist high, but which was locked with a slide bolt from the inside. [The group was] in general disrupting activities of the board."

Also in Laud's FBI file are eight snapshots photographed inside the draft board offices, obviously taken by a government undercover operative. Although Humphreys's face is not recognizable in any of the photographs, at least three close-up shots taken from behind him clearly show that it is indeed Laud who is leading the protestors and that he is dressed in clerical garb.

On May 7 Laud was arrested and was taken to the Alton, Illinois, Police Department to be fingerprinted and photographed. On that same day he was taken to court and posted a bond of fifteen hundred dollars. On May 26 he was indicted by a federal grand jury for destruction of federal property and violation of the Selective Service Act. On June 11 he appeared in the U.S. District Court in Alton.

The FBI noted to the Secret Service that Laud Humphreys had made "expressions of strong or violent anti-U.S. sentiment." The FBI also noted: "Prior acts (including arrests or convictions) or conduct or statements indicating a propensity for violence and antipathy toward good order and government." The only entry in Laud's FBI file prior to the demonstration at SIU was the entry about his complaint regarding the racially segregated restaurant in Memphis, Tennessee. This complaint apparently rose to the level of "strong, anti-U.S. sentiment." An anonymous member of the Southern Illinois University–Edwardsville (SIU–E) academic community "who has furnished reliable information in the past, advised in January, 1970, that Laud [was] a sponsor of the Committee for International Concern [CIC] on the campus of SIU–E and has been active in promoting activities of [the] Vietnam Moratorium Committee within the Committee for International Concern." This informant at SIU told the FBI that "Humphreys has definitely moved the philosophy and motives of the group to the left of center and has been obscene and vituperative in remarks concerning the present administration and United States policies." An informant also noted that CIC "has entertained representatives from other left wing groups like the Students for a Democratic Society (SDS) and the Young Socialist Alliance (YSA)" as well as the Marxist-Leninist, Progressive Labor Party (PLP). The file observed that the SDS "advocate[s] that an alliance between workers and students is vital to the bringing about of a revolution in the United States." On the basis of all this, Laud was added to the FBI's "Agitator Index" on June 8. Moreover, his file was coded by the FBI as a foreign counterintelligence matter. And consistent with this label it was noted that Humphreys was the SIU faculty adviser to the campus Youth International Party (YIP).

On hearing of Laud's new position at the State University of New York (SUNY) in Albany, beginning in the fall of 1970, the FBI sought to determine if "there is a source in a responsible position in the State University of New York to whom copies" of Laud's file could be transmitted. At this time it was observed that the FBI office in "Springfield (Illinois) is considering counterintelligence action against Humphreys in connection with his forthcoming position at the State University of New York." What type of counterintelligence might have been contemplated for criminals who break pictures of presidents was not specified, nor was the significance of his forthcoming position in New York. The FBI noted that it had located someone at the State University of New York who had agreed to provide information to them on Humphreys on a confidential basis. In any case, this federal program used infiltration of dissident groups, extralegal violence, and harassment through the legal system (Glick 1989). Threats of violence had been used against Laud and his family, the student protest group he led had been infiltrated, and the legal system had been used against him in a heavy-handed way in order to silence him. On December 2, 1970, Humphreys was brought to trial in Springfield and the next day changed his plea from not guilty to guilty as a result of a plea bargain. In federal court in Springfield he was given a one-year sentence—the first three months in jail and the balance suspended—and placed on three years' probation.

Official Court Records of Trial and Appeals

During pretrial hearings (August 26, 1970) Laud's attorney, Richard Shaikewitz, moved that the judge recuse himself from the case because the judge's son had been wounded while working as a journalist in Vietnam. The judge refused, saying: "Every defendant always gets a fair and impartial trial in this court." A draft board employee testified that the demonstrators entered a door to the office that said "No Admittance," many of them carrying tambourines while they were shouting slogans and singing. Humphreys stood on a desk and tore up a memorandum. Laud's attorney asked for a continuance to show that the picture frame was made of plastic and thus clearly was not worth the one hundred dollars required for a felony charge. For his part, Laud argued that the situation required drastic action since students throughout the nation were quite distressed about the draft, the war, and the killings at Kent State. The judge countered: "I've read this probation report, you used inappropriate language, was it necessary for you to use that language?" (Sentencing Hearing, January 7, 1971). Precisely what type of language the judge might have thought appropriate to use in protesting genocide in Southeast Asia is beyond our knowledge.

The judge was again asked to recuse himself on August 26, 1970, to which the judge responded: "Well, I don't see where anything that happened to my son would have anything to do with this man. My son was a war correspondent; he wasn't a soldier." Later Humphreys's attorney argued that Laud had not violated the Selective Service Act of 1967 because there had been no declaration of war, and this made the operation of the Selective Service Board illegal. Mr. Shaikewitz also asked the court to determine the size of the photo of the president and its makeup in order to determine its value, for, as noted above, if it was worth less than one hundred dollars the defendant could not be charged with a felony. He also requested the time of all Selective Service Board coffee breaks, for if they were on break when the demonstrators arrived in the office their work could not have been disrupted. All these motions were denied.

One of the draft board employees testified that Humphreys was indeed in the draft board offices during the protest and was dressed as a clergyman. The witness also testified to being frightened by the crowd and that Laud had read a memorandum requiring an increase in the quota to be drafted that month, and then afterward tore it into many pieces. Another witness recalled that the protestors used "obscene chants" and that "one girl standing very close to me said, 'let's burn the files.'" Humphreys admitted to reading the memorandum and also to the destruction of Nixon's picture for its "symbolic value." His FBI files indicate that an unidentified undercover government operative among the demonstrators took at least nine photographs of the demonstrators, clearly identifying many in the crowd but with no clear pictures of Laud's face.

Motions were made to determine whether any undercover agents were among the protestors, the alleged dollar value of the destroyed memo, the size of the photograph of Nixon, the exact cost of the photograph, the cost of the frame, the precise verbal utterances of the defendant, an explanation of why the defendant was selected for prosecution when many others were shown in the undercover photos, and the names and addresses of all undercover operatives involved because there may have been elements of entrapment. Humphreys's attorney also requested a copy of Laud's FBI file and argued in a motion that if it existed, this constituted a violation of his right to privacy guaranteed by the U.S. Constitution. All motions were denied.

On January 7, 1971, Mr. Shaikewitz filed a motion to stay the sentencing in part, because "the destruction of a photograph with a value that does not exceed [even] $1.00 must be measured against the damage that might have occurred given the mood of the crowd. The burning of files, for example." And on March 6, 1972, the judge sustained the prosecution's objection to the defense argument that, in other areas at the time, draft files had been burned. The prosecutor also said; "I think the Court should also note that the Federal Government does have a very vital interest in deterring this kind of conduct. . . . Your Honor, I think Mr. Humphreys is the kind of individual we expect a higher degree of conduct from." Laud countered: "I strongly believe in this instance that the only type of behavior that giving me a jail sentence would deter would be for persons to stand forward with courage on the campuses of our universities and try to prevent violence." Finally, Laud's attorney asked that the court "state the reasons for the sentence." The judge refused, which was consistent with an earlier refusal to release the presentence report. Presentence reports were held to be confidential based as they often were on the testimony of government informants.

In 1972 Humphreys appealed his jail sentence to the U.S. Court of Appeals for the Seventh Circuit. The court heard testimony from draft board employees indicating that Humphreys was indeed the leader of the crowd of student demonstrators and that he had appeared in clergyman's attire. For his part, during these proceedings, Laud argued that he had done a "good deed" (U.S. Court of Appeals 1972, 244) by steering students away from campus buildings to the downtown draft board, implying that there could have been destruction of campus property. He also argued that by destroying the picture of the president he engaged in a "symbolic protest" making violence among the students less likely (244).

The original felony charge had been dropped in exchange for Humphreys's guilty plea, and thus he faced a maximum of one year in prison. As noted earlier, his sentence was actually only three months in a local jail. This was the sentence that Laud appealed, arguing that he should not serve any term of confinement. The Appeals Court reminded

Humphreys on six different occasions that he could withdraw his guilty plea. But Laud recognized the risks of even greater punishment involved in a new trial and declined these offers. Laud also argued that "extraordinary circumstances" required his actions and that his sentence amounted to "cruel and unusual punishment" (U.S. Court of Appeals 1972, 245–46). Both of these arguments were denied by the Appeals Court and Laud's sentence was affirmed. He also asked to see his presentence reports on which his sentence was based. This request was denied by the court to protect "confidential informants whose testimony is included in the report . . . [including] trustworthy local informants, persons close to the accused" (245).

Prior to sentencing Laud asked many friends, colleagues, and associates to write to the judge requesting that he sentence Laud to probation. The typical argument was that his leadership of the students greatly reduced the threat of violence on the campus. The SIU chancellor's letter made this argument (Rendleman 1970), as did letters from the chancellor's Assistant for Legal Affairs (Davis 1970) and from Oklahoma Senator Fred Harris (1970). Other letters to the judge emphasized the quality of Humphreys's intellectual contributions. Lee Rainwater, now at Harvard, stressed this factor (1970), as did Herbert Gans (1970) of MIT and American Sociological Association President William Sewell (1970). All of Humphreys's colleagues in the School of Criminal Justice at the State University of New York at Albany (Wilkins 1970) also wrote letters on his behalf. Irving Louis Horowitz (1970) wrote to the judge asking for leniency, making a special plea based on the fact that Laud's wife was blind and that rearing their two children alone would create a terrible burden.

State University at Albany and One Summer in Jail

Armed with the C. Wright Mills Award in 1970, Humphreys moved to a major research university and was promoted to associate professor after only two years as an assistant professor. He joined the School of Criminal Justice at SUNY–Albany from 1970 to 1972. Almost immediately on arriving in Albany Humphreys developed a serious confrontation with a senior professor, Hans Toch, such that Laud soon felt that once again he had to move on (Henslin 2001b). Rainwater agreed (2001): "I remember Laud talking about disagreements with Toch. . . . Toch's take on criminology was very conservative and they argued about that. Toch was opposed to [Laud's] continuing at Albany."

For his part, Hans Toch recalled (2001): "Laud Humphreys was hired here as a tenured associate professor. I urged that we bring him here after I heard him give a presentation at the ASA meetings in San Francisco. He gave a terrific talk at the meetings and afterwards that prompted me to read his very creative book. I team-taught a criminology course with him once. He was much more radical in his views than me and we took turns lecturing and gave critical comments and dialogue during the other's presentations. He served three months in the Albany County jail for his anti-Vietnam war activities in Illinois. His colleagues at SUNY-Albany supported him through all of this but he wanted to live in California." Thus after two years at Albany Humphreys accepted a position as associate professor at Pitzer College. In 1975 he was promoted to professor and remained in this position until his retirement in 1986.

For removing a picture of Richard Nixon from the wall and breaking it over his knee, he was arrested, tried, and convicted of destruction of federal property, and received a sentence which he served during the summer of 1972. Laud's daughter, Clair, who was seven years old at the time, recalled that she drew a chalk picture of a clown to help cheer up her father, but it was not allowed in prison. "Laud had nightmares about his stay in jail" (Miller 2001a). Humphreys wrote (1975, 225): "I was arrested, tried, and imprisoned under Mitchell's authority for destroying a photograph of Nixon during a draft board demonstration in 1970."

During his first semester in Albany Laud wrote an essay for a gay rights magazine in San Francisco on the sexuality of Jesus (Humphreys 1970c, 13): "Were the Church's official teaching to be believed, his penis would surely have atrophied for lack of use by the age of 33. . . . In the years of my parochial ministry, I used to shock people by suggesting that the doctrine of the incarnation necessitated our recognizing that 'the God we worship wet his pants, defecated, and had to have his diapers changed.' Had I proceeded with the logical extension of this central, Christian doctrine to proclaim that Jesus 'jacked off' as a teenager, my active ministry would never have lasted ten years."

Not content with this inflammatory rhetoric, Laud continued (Humphreys 1970c, 14, 38): "Paul was the closet queen most influential in corrupting what had the beginnings of a perfectly good religion. Paul is the one who urged Christians to put on 'the breastplate of righteousness' [and thus] . . . a student of the Gospels might conclude that Jesus, if not actively gay, at least gave evidence of homosexual feelings. The Fourth Gospel, supposedly written by John, states repeatedly and quite pointedly that John was the disciple 'whom Jesus loved' and who sat with his head resting on Jesus' chest at the Last Supper. . . . The Church insists that he was completely human [thus] he cannot have fought off erections all his life."

Another New Home at Pitzer College

In January 1972 Humphreys wrote to Glenn Goodwin asking about the possibility of a teaching post at Pitzer College (Humphreys 1972a). Laud explained that he preferred the California climate, teaching in a sociology department rather than criminal justice, and contact with liberal arts undergraduates. Humphreys landed on his feet at Pitzer in Claremont, California, and was doing well there for most of the decade. "It was while incarcerated that he signed a contract to come to Pitzer College" (*Claremont Courier* 1988). Friends recalled (Goodwin, Horowitz, and Nardi 1991, 144) that "Laud negotiated his contract with Pitzer's Dean of Faculty (also a sociologist) from a prison pay phone and his wife, Nancy, smuggled the contract into the prison for his signature." Albert Schwartz (2001), the sociologist and at the time (1971–77) Dean of the Faculty, recalled: "I wasn't concerned that we hired Laud from jail. As it turned out I had no problems with Laud while I was Dean. I didn't see any signs of him beginning to turn the corner. Although some students complained about his courses he still packed in 100 students in each of his classes, which is four times the average size at Pitzer."

A colleague at Pitzer, Rudi Volti (2001), noted: "Laud officiated at my wedding to Ann Stromberg in September 1976. Ann especially was very close to Laud and Nancy, for they were a kind of surrogate family to her when she came to Pitzer. He routinely taught a course titled Stigmatized Sexual Behavior. After a few years we felt the course was causing difficulty for the Sociology Field Group and for the college as a whole. So we requested that he cease teaching the course. Laud was experiencing difficulties due to his drinking and Nancy's deteriorating health. In my view, Laud achieved greatness too early in his career, like Joseph Heller with *Catch-22*. He never again came close to such great work. He continued to teach a course on the prison experience. He made the most out of the time he served, three months that he arranged to serve during the summer break."

Ann Stromberg (2001) admitted that, "Laud's interest in the Sociology Field Group activities at Pitzer ebbed and flowed over time. Eventually he cut back on his involvement in the college and in his research. You have to give him credit that, the last few years of his life he was sober. He talked with me several times about his anniversaries of being clean and sober. Laud typically taught Methods of Field Research [in spite of his methods being widely censured in the discipline], The Prison Experience, Seminar on Crime and Mass Society, and Stigmatized Sexual Behavior. It was this last course that caused some trouble due to complaints from some students and parents." His 1983 vita (Appendix A) also shows that he taught Introduction to Sociology, Social Problems, Sociology of Deviance, Social Sources of Violence, and Subcultures and Occupations.

A Second Book: *Out of the Closets*

In 1972 Humphreys published his second and final book, a textbook covering the history and patterns of discrimination against gays and lesbians, as well as their resistance to this oppression, entitled *Out of the Closets: The Sociology of Homosexual Liberation*. He began one chapter with this quote: "San Francisco is a refugee camp for homosexuals" (Humphreys 1972b, 13). He noted that in forty-five of the fifty states there was no legal homosexual outlet, "but Connecticut, Colorado, Idaho, and Oregon were added that year [1971] to Illinois as states removing the criminal stigma from consensual sodomy between adults" (7–8). On the other hand, federal employment could be terminated for allegations of being a security risk by refusing to submit to blackmail, if extortionists report the victim to the government. The only safe occupations were those such as hairdresser and interior decorator. Certainly membership in the armed services was (and still is) not safe. If one reports their homosexual preference, they will be excluded from the armed services, but this will become a part of their permanent public record. If they do not report their sexual preference and it is later revealed, they can be given a less-than-honorable discharge. On the other hand, it should be noted that if they are closeted they run the risk of being "outed" and suffering beatings or death at the hands of fellows soldiers (*Washington Post* 1999). Laud's book concludes with a list of demands including, "Issuance by the President of an executive order prohibiting the military from excluding [any person] for reasons of their sexual orientation" (166). More than three decades later this is still far from a reality.

Attempting to pass as straight takes a heavy toll on an individual's self-worth. "It is true even today that anyone openly associating with homosexuals or protecting them from harassment himself runs the risk of falling under suspicion of being homosexual" (Humphreys 1972b, 53). Humphreys continues arguing that, "the liberal mind recoils in thinking of oppression. . . . But dominant Americans reject any implication that they might be bullies; and, even when scorned as weak and sissy, homosexuals are seldom seen as innocent" (14). In response to oppression the homosexual subculture appears to specialize in a "genius for style innovation, for new art forms" (73); it also "heightens sensitivity" (74) and "humanism" (76), and helps to create a special "flair" (77). Indeed, "skills all oppressed groups tend to develop may be classified as *street skills*" (66).

Out of the Closets covers topics such as the Christopher Street riots at the Stonewall Inn; forms of oppression, including the law; gays in prison and the military; the Gay Rights movement; skills of the oppressed, including passing as straight; and confronting homosexual stigma in the churches. In the fall of 1970 Black Panther leader Huey Newton wrote that those in the Gay Liberation Front (GLF) were both friends and potential allies. Yet GLF members were ejected from meetings when they attempted to attend that winter's Black Panther convention.

Martin Weinberg reviewed *Out of the Closets* for *Contemporary Sociology*. While praising the author's vivid sociological imagination, creativity, and literary talents there is, Weinberg noted, "a tendency toward overstatement and a lack of adequate support for a number of the generalizations offered" (1974, 264). The book "exaggerates homosexuals' 'special talents' and is incorrect on various points" (265). According to Weinberg's assessment, research has not shown that homosexuals are more creative and innovative than others, necessarily superior in skills of pastoral care, nor unmatched in their dexterity in political organizing— all claims made in the book.

The Los Angeles *Advocate*, a newspaper addressing the needs and interests of the gay community, gave the book a positive evaluation (Doyle 1973, 40): "It would be difficult to imagine that a steadier, more persuasive voice could be found to speak in support of gay hopes and aspirations than that of Laud Humphreys. Viewing our difficulties from the outside . . . Laud Humphreys and his family live in Claremont, California." While the review is positive, it does note that this is an evaluation from the "outside" and emphasized that while Laud was a friend of the gay community he was clearly not part of the gay community, living as he did with his family.

The Influence of *Out of the Closets*

Warren and DeLora (1978) discuss the Gay Students' Union (GSU) at a "Western" public state university and the opposition of this campus group to the university ROTC program. In all such programs Warren and DeLora note that there is financial cooperation between universities and the military. The universities provide ROTC with office space and secretarial support; in turn, the ROTC provides the students enrolled in the program with scholarships, books, and uniforms. The gay students were "interested in highlighting the general discrimination against gays by the military and by society" (72). The GSU asked that student government support a move to suspend the campus ROTC program until homosexuals were provided the same legal protections in ROTC as guaranteed to any other minority. Student government agreed. The GSU then planned to picket military recruiters on campus. Unfortunately the university faculty and administration did not support the GSU demands, and the ROTC program was not forced to alter its policies or to disband. This demonstrates the failure of gays to attract other oppressed groups as allies. In *Out of the Closets* (1972b) Humphreys could find no evidence of success in gay coalition building, and clearly in this instance the GSU had only limited success in building political bridges.

Herman and Musolf (1998) studied personal resistance among former psychiatric patients in their attempts to control their public identities. The study involved 285 former Canadian mental patients. There are, in fact, "rituals of resistance" (432). These former patients generally define police, mental health workers, and neighbors as the "enemy" (434). Therefore they often decide to moon such people, to spit on them, or to draw graffiti on such buildings as mental hospitals. Many also refused to work in sheltered workshop settings or joined activist groups for former mental patients to attempt political action. "Ex-mental patient activists conceived of their problems not as personal failings or potentially stigmatizing attributes but, rather, as societal problems" (444), and the authors noted that Humphreys in *Out of the Closets* referred to this as "stigma conversion."

Herman (1993) also studied stigma management of former psychiatric patients. Patients learned of their initial labeling from a variety of sources, including police, clergy, physicians, family, or friends. Not totally dissimilar to tearoom participants, some former psychiatric patients attempted to conceal their devalued attribute, in their case by withdrawing or attempting to conceal their illness. In *Out of the Closets* (1972b, 138) Humphreys noted that "passing is the type of stigma evasion most common to homosexuals. . . . [T]his 'closet queen' method of adapting creates a number of difficulties when it comes to organizing homosexuals for social change. . . . Closet queens cannot be expected to greet the call to gay pride with enthusiasm," thereby weakening any possibility of political coalition. In any case, *Out of the Closets* had only a minimal impact compared to *Tearoom Trade*.

Coming Out

Laud Humphreys came out at the 1974 American Sociological Association meetings in an emotional exchange with Edward Sagarin, with Laud's wife, Nancy, sitting in the audience. Sagarin had been a closeted gay man and had written in defense of the gay community under the pseudonym of Donald Webster Cory. Later, he had decided he was straight and accused gay researchers of dishonesty and a lack of objectivity. Sagarin (1974, 31) presented a paper that read in part: "The theme of . . . Humphreys and others is: Come out, come out, wherever you are. . . . I can tell you: they will be in another box, in another closet, imprisoned in their homosexuality. To come out and to accept gay identity is not freedom. On the contrary, it is the greatest possible renunciation of freedom. . . . Homosexuality . . . is a characteristic, not a condition. There are no homosexuals. There are only people who behave homosexually at various times of their lives. . . . Homosexuality is real, but the homosexual is an invention; it is an invention believed in so thoroughly by some people that they become what they were improperly tagged as being." Sagarin was especially critical of researchers such as Humphreys who have "enthusiasm in urging others to make great sacrifices, very careful delineation of the fact that their own lives are untainted by the behavior that they so courageously defend (in others)."

Humphreys recalled: "I blew his cover. 'Accidentally' addressing him as Professor Cory. I said, before that audience of my peers, 'I want to be honest with you and I want you to know that I am gay. I have done my research and written my book *[Tearoom Trade]* as a gay person, closeted, trying to come out of that closet, dealing with my own personal pain. Now I want to ask Professor Cory—I mean Sagarin—to be honest with us. Never has he identified his research population—he's just always said that we are lying. I want to know who he has studied.' When I finished the whole audience rose in a standing ovation. I was crying. Then Sagarin got up to give his rebuttal. He burst into tears and all he could say between sobs was 'I am my data.' They called it Monday, Bloody Monday" (Gross 1993, 17).

Indeed, "Nancy was in the audience that day. She found out about it the same moment that everyone else did. Her initial reaction was supportive" (Miller 2001a). After coming out Laud felt free to discuss his own sexuality in the classroom because it was relevant to the courses he taught (Lazere 1987, 16): "I walk into a class and say, 'I'm a cock-sucker and I'm a drunk and I'm an addict—all things that you have been taught are terrible. Now let's talk about these things.'"

The issue of objectivity and sexual orientation is of profound importance and far from settled. The question is, must one be gay to study gays? This is a matter of perspective that social science applies in one way to those who study race and gender but differently to those who study poverty or criminal behavior such as homicide and rape. In the case of felons or the poor, it is generally reasoned that you don't have to be one to know one. Brian Miller (2001a) argued: "Laud was interested in marginals because he was marginal. . . . He felt, however, that his marriage and his tearoom research stigmatized him in the gay world. Several gay activists told him that his tearoom research embarrassed them, that it unnecessarily publicized a minor and insignificant part of homosexuality and put all homosexuals in a bad light. Worse, they felt, by being married and doing research on gays, Laud was merely 'slumming' in gay territory."

Anthropologist Joseph Carrier recalled that he met Humphreys in 1975 and that they remained in close contact for the next five years until he left Los Angeles for employment elsewhere. "Since anthropology faculty positions in Los Angeles were impossible to find at the time, Laud gave me half of his consulting business evaluating juvenile delinquency prevention programs." Such an incredibly generous offer of sharing his wealth was typical of Humphreys, dating back to his first year out of the seminary. For approximately five years they were quite close, with Carrier serving as Humphreys's "confidant" (Carrier 2001). Carrier has recently written about the ethical trials of gay men conducting research on male homosexuality (1999, 208): "The major fear is that the gay male researcher may be diverted by uncontrollable sexual urges and target male respondents as sexual partners during the field investigation." Carrier explains that celibacy is not an option because the fieldwork can stretch over several years. Other problems involve the urges of respondents in participant-observation studies. Having stated these special ethical problems does not necessarily move us closer to their solution.

In any event, regarding the critics of his book, Humphreys concluded: "In the short run, they caused a lot of stress, which was compounded by the fact that I was also coming out as 'bisexual.' Finally I rallied enough self-respect to admit I was gay. Some friends feared this admission would totally discredit the research, but my candor worked to the contrary. It gave the research more credence, since people now knew I was both academically and personally knowledgeable about tearooms" (Miller 1982, 39). Here Laud comes close to admitting that he knew those who frequented tearooms as both an observer and a participant.

Leaving Home

Laud recognized what had happened: "My wife, however, was upset by these developments. We tried to work out a compromise, but as I became more openly gay, the marriage deteriorated. By this time I wasn't going to tearooms anymore, but it finally registered with my wife that I was more in love with another man than with her, and she asked me to leave. We divorced two years later. I still have weekly visits with my two teen-age kids" (Miller 1982, 39). Again we see the near admission of being a participant in tearooms, not a mere observer. In any case, Laud left home to live with Brian Miller in the summer of 1978. Miller (2001a) recalled that in April 1980: "Laud was given divorce papers by a server at our apartment at 6:30 A.M." Miller also remembered that Laud did not secure a good financial settlement with the divorce in spite of having hired a divorce attorney.

Clair had painful memories of all this: "I was in high school when my father left home and he was proud of who he was—it was hard for me to have everyone in school know that my dad had left home to live with a man. I was bitter about Brian Miller who I felt that by moving in with my father attempted to enhance himself with Laud's fame" (Beller 2001). Whatever the truth of this matter, Laud did serve on Brian's Ph.D. dissertation committee as an outside reader at the University of Alberta and was very generous with his help to Brian. Just how generous is not known, but for a long time Brian was unable to finish his dissertation until Laud joined his committee. Miller (2001a) reports that originally, since Laud was approximately twenty years his senior, "I didn't think of him in sexual terms, but as I found out later, he was interested in me."

According to Carrier (2001): "At the very least the relationship with Brian was not good for Laud personally or professionally. Laud took Brian to faculty parties and danced with Brian and pushed this relationship in the face of his colleagues and college administrators. Although Laud in truth could be suffocating in his relationships, he believed that Brian was dating other men, yet for a time he still allowed Brian to live

in his house. Laud had other unhappy experiences with those he be-
friended. One of Laud's other acquaintances that he had sponsored for
a faculty position revealed to Nancy that Laud was a practicing homosexual and forced the breakup in the marriage. For years Nancy must
have known that Laud was gay or at least bisexual, but didn't know that
he was a sexually active homosexual. This revelation could not have
come at a worse time for Nancy since she had just lost her eyesight due
to diabetes. Laud had indicated that this diabetes ultimately made child-
bearing impossible for Nancy."

Just prior to leaving Nancy, Laud went on a diet and lost more than
fifty pounds and bought a "new sporty Datsun Z. Nancy saw this as his
mid-life crisis, but it was more than that" (Miller 2001a). Soon his phy-
sician told Laud that he should stop smoking since he had numerous
respiratory problems, including colds, coughing, and mouth sores. Laud
cut back from four to two packs a day and soon started smoking a pipe
(Miller 2001a). By 1979 Laud "sold the family home and bought a condo
for Nancy and the kids in Claremont. It was hard for them to give up
their beautiful suburban neighborhood. The divorce caused more financial problems and he took on more jobs (evaluation of diversion projects,
expert witnesses in court cases) to make ends meet" (Miller 2001a). Fred
Lynch (2001b) also noted that Laud lost a lot of weight after he left
home since he was now more concerned with being sexually attractive.
Lynch also agreed that Laud "had a great deal of trouble living within
his means. Given his spendthrift ways Nancy's aunt Eleanor had set up
a financial trust for Nancy that she could draw on only a little at a time.
On a number of occasions Laud and Nancy tried to break Eleanor's trust
to get at all the money, but they were never successful."

In 1978 Humphreys published an interview with Evelyn Hooker, the
pioneering psychologist who began the systematic study of gay men
during the 1950s. Laud quoted Hooker as saying: "I think the major
changes which have occurred are not in the area of personality dynamics
or of the adjustment of individuals, but in the questions which concern
gay people in their social setting. . . . [T]he interplay between the two
sets of variables—those of personality dynamics and social variables—is
essential. So if one wants to understand the behavior of gay men, for instance, one has not only to understand individual dynamics, one has
also to understand the milieu in which they live" (Humphreys 1978,
197). This is just what Humphreys had done in his dissertation research,
though many of his subjects were heterosexually identified men engaged in homosexual behavior rather than gay men per se. Hooker was

also quoted as saying that to study this milieu the appearance of gay researchers had been essential. As a woman she could do research in "every place gay men go, except gay baths and tearooms" (198). This limitation, she observed, also applies to anyone who is straight.

In 1979 Laud published a short essay as part of an introductory sociology textbook (Humphreys 1979a). Here he noted that approximately a quarter of a million persons identified as homosexuals were murdered in the Nazi death camps. He also observed that American public opinion polls routinely indicated that most citizens do not approve of homosexual behavior and that this condemnation is reflected in state laws prohibiting homosexual acts between consenting adults. In this society, Laud correctly observed, all individuals who do not claim a homosexual identity are assumed by default to be heterosexual. Yet, even in the face of this oppression and social pressure, some people come out and proclaim a gay identity. And no amount of conditioning can change this basic identity.

In this essay Humphreys brings up an old adversary—Edward Sagarin. Sagarin claimed that people become trapped in identities and that those who think they are gay suffer from mistaken identities. Laud noted that Sagarin referred to this as "the tyranny of isness" (Humphreys 1979a, 239). Laud reasoned, however, that for gay people the tyranny of isness is "less appalling than the tyranny of isn'tness" (242).

In 1979 Humphreys also published "Exodus and Identity: The Emerging Gay Culture," in which he writes: "With the beginning of gay liberation in the Christopher Street riots, a marked transfiguration became observable in the gay world" (Humphreys 1979b, 136). "When a cultural entity becomes extensive and diverse—when it is seen to spawn subcultures of its own—we use the term 'satellite culture' to designate it. . . . Another characteristic of satellite cultures is that each has a history of persecution, an exodus out of bondage into the Promised Land" (140). "Satellite cultures do not just emerge; they break free. As the bonds of oppression are broken, the shabby garments of deviant subcultures are also shed. . . . While organizing for power, gays have also facilitated emergence of a proud satellite culture by raising consciousness" (142). He also noted: "On the wall of my study hangs a copy of an advertisement by the Gay Student Union, which recently filled half a page of a large university newspaper. It lists the names of a hundred homosexual notables, from Alexander the Great and Horatio Alger to Virginia Woolf and Zeno" (143).

Humphreys published three articles in 1980, with Brian Miller, demonstrating that their relationship was both sexual and intellectual. In a book edited by Judd Marmor the two published a paper entitled "Identities in the Emerging Gay Culture," in which they discussed the importance of "gay scenes" to this development (Humphreys and Miller 1980, 144). Miller and Humphreys had published "Keeping in Touch," a piece about reconnecting with gay fathers that had been used in earlier research by Brian Miller and Laud's tearoom participants for purposes of longitudinal study. Careful reading of the newspapers during the year following the tearoom data collection found that one participant had become a candidate for a "rightist party and another assumed a position of leadership in a League for Decent Literature" (Miller and Humphreys 1980a, 217). Brian Miller found that 12 percent of gay fathers eventually became active in gay organizations.

Another paper was published in *Qualitative Sociology*, where Miller and Humphreys claimed that, in the gay community, "contrary to popular belief, we found no deaths resulting from sado-masochistic sex play" (Miller and Humpreys 1980b, 175). And also contrary to some claims, "Movement of homosexual marginals into openly gay lifestyles appears to *decrease* their vulnerability to violent crime" (182). Humphreys had been working on this research for some time prior to its eventual publication. In 1975 he had described the main outlines of the investigation to a *New York Times* reporter: "Society's attitude toward homosexuals causes some people to feel that they have the right to beat up gays, and people who fear they are homosexuals are sometimes filled with so much self-hatred that they develop psychotic patterns that can lead them to murder" (*New York Times* 1975, 14).

Humphreys wrote a stinging 1980 review, published in *Trans-action*, of *Homosexuality in Perspective* by the eminent sex research team of William Masters and Virginia Johnson. In the review he compares their book to the work of Caesar Lombroso and is amused that the prominent researchers were surprised by the great similarities between gay and straight respondents. He noted, "Homosexuals do not ejaculate out of their ears or have orgasmic contractions of the sinus cavities but climax like everyone else" (Humphreys 1980b, 85).

6

The Long (and Rapid) Road Down

Laud's Last Book Project

In 1980 Humphreys took a sabbatical and began a book on moral entrepreneurs, on what he referred to as the "breastplate of righteousness" (Miller 2001b). He never completed this book, and the manuscript, entitled "Immoral Crusaders," is located in the One Institute and Archives in Los Angeles. The chapters and some of their content are summarized below.

Chapter 1. Moral Crusaders

The book begins with the study's major premise: "Self-righteous crusaders are really sinners in sheep's clothing. They are flawed by a split between their sex lives and their affections. This split generates the intensity behind their moral crusades. . . . [T]he Moralists are actually moral violators in disguise. The very transgressions they denounce from their pulpits and seats of authority are sins they commit in private. . . . Sex, for the Righteous Ones, is a curse. . . . What they will not let themselves enjoy must also be forbidden for others, which helps explain why sex is one of the first things Moral Crusaders attack." This psychological model is Laud's dubious explanation for almost everything on the political Right. "Crusaders, we shall discover, are always hypocrites. But their hypocrisy takes on an intensity that distinguishes them from the rest of us hypocrites. We all project our failings onto others, but few think it necessary to condemn, imprison or execute those who fail to

live up to moral standards we ourselves secretly violate." All the con-
demnations of these leaders are actually "smokescreens."

Chapter 2. Upright on Clay Feet

This chapter, like the others, consists solely of deviant case histories.
For example, Humphreys recounts how a member of his parish, who
was a conservative district attorney, was hospitalized after being involved in an extremely serious auto accident. With his life hanging in
the balance, this man confessed to Laud that he had often frequented
prostitutes for sado-masochistic acts. He and his wife had slept in separate rooms for years. Humphreys contends that this man's hatred for
antiwar protestors and liberals was generated by his loveless sex life.
This Nixon supporter had a "catalogue of enemies," not just individuals
who opposed the Vietnam War, but he condemned minority groups
"en masse: Blacks or Jews or the Irish, Gays, Catholics." Similarly, a conservative Youth for Christ minister had affairs with young girls because
of problems in his marital sex life. Some moral crusaders are celibate;
others are child molesters or experience some form of compulsive sex.
Charles Manson used sex to "brainwash, dominate, manipulate, and ex-
ploit others. Such use of sex to control others is a common characteristic of Moral Crusaders." Manson portrayed Blacks as enemies and in-
ferior to the white race. "This blending of religious fundamentalism and
political absolutism is readily apparent in the Ayatollah Khomeini. . . .
He is both Holy Man and revolutionary, dictator and spiritual leader.
[Similarly] Hitler saw himself as both Führer and Savior of his people."

Chapter 3. Sex, Celibacy, and Politics

Humphreys reports on a 1948 meeting in a hotel room with a leading
politician from South Carolina, while Laud was an undergraduate at
the University of Virginia and a reporter for the student newspaper, *The
Cavalier Daily*. This political leader had been invited to speak on the
Virginia campus. Humphreys was ushered into the room, finding only
the political leader and his wife. He was invited to join the politician
and his wife for a sexual threesome. During this interview, this "tall
standard bearer of the States' Rights Democratic Party was clad only in
a towel—his wife in her slip. 'Ain't she got a pretty ass?' he asked me
with a wink. 'Now you young folks just get comfortable while I shower
a bit.' With her husband out of the room, [she] explained to me—with
no little embarrassment, I thought—what her husband liked to do. She

sat on the arm of my chair and loosened my tie, explaining that [he] liked to be the third person in bed with his wife and a young man." Laud declined the invitation.

It is worth nothing that this archconservative longtime segregation-ist served as U.S. Senator from South Carolina from 1954 until shortly before his death in 2003. "He neither smoked nor drank, [but] was known for fondling women in the Senate elevators" (*New York Times* 2003a). He was twice married and at the time of his death was separated from his second wife who had been quoted as saying that she wanted "some measure of independence." She was a former Miss South Caro-lina, who was forty-four years his junior. Although his opposition to ra-cial integration was legendary, shortly after his death his African Amer-ican daughter first made her lineage known (*New York Times* 2003b). The senator never publicly acknowledged her existence. Laud Hum-phreys could have had no idea of the extent of this official's hypocrisy at the time Laud served as a campus newspaper reporter in 1948, or even as late as 1980 when beginning his third book.

Humphreys continues by pointing out that J. Edgar Hoover, the long-time FBI Director, had great contempt for the Rev. Martin Lu-ther King and did what he could to undermine support for this Nobel Prize–winning civil rights leader. Hoover also disliked women and never married, but he had a male companion for much of his adult life. Hoover apparently hated the idea of sex and hated those who enjoyed it. In addition to those like Hoover who hate sex, Humphreys argued that pedophiles are likely to become Moral Crusaders and that this was true of actor Errol Flynn and the creator of the cartoon *Li'l Abner*, Al Capp, both of whom were reputed to be right-wing racists.

Chapter 4. Impersonal Sex

Two examples are especially noteworthy. A right-wing state congress-man from Pennsylvania died of a heart attack in 1978 in a Miami gay bath while in the nude. It was later determined that for years he had sexual encounters in highway restrooms. G. Harold Carswell, who was a federal judge nominated for the U.S. Supreme Court by Nixon in 1970 and then rejected by the Senate, was arrested for attempting to have sex with a vice squad officer in plainclothes. According to Humphreys, the problem with "bisexuals" such as this state legislator and judge is that, "in general, men who present themselves as bisexual are desperately concerned with escaping a homosexual identity—one they fear and abhor. While rejecting their own sexuality, they also avoid heterosexual relationships. Their version of the sex/love rift is one that avoids commitment and emphasizes impersonal encounters."

Chapter 5. The Bible on the Table . . . and the Footsie under It

Now the chapters begin to seem less complete than the first four. In chapter 5 Laud focuses on publicly pious fundamentalist Christian crusaders whose private lives are punctuated by perversions. The chapter mixes data from newspaper accounts of scandalized preachers, Humphreys's personal observations of Oklahoma tent revivals when he was a youth, and a personal interview with a small-town faith healer who resigned from his ministry after a sexual scandal. Humphreys describes these preachers as exploiting members of their congregations both monetarily and sexually. He mentions "millionaire crusaders" and illustrates such ministers with the case of the Rev. Jim Bakker, who, by coincidence, was later forced from his lucrative ministry by his sexual indiscretions. Humphreys also discusses how the Rev. Billy James Hargis was disgraced in the 1970s and forced out of his lucrative Tulsa ministry because of accusations of a series of affairs with young men.

Chapter 6. Secrets in the Sacristy

Here Humphreys describes the rigidly conservative Episcopal Bishop of Colorado who was forced to resign in disgrace once it was disclosed that this leading cleric was consorting with female prostitutes. What was surprising about this case was that the bishop "became a symbol of rigidity and unrelieved orthodoxy during the years he governed Colorado's Episcopal Church. He was strict on moral issues, strict on adherence to orthodox doctrine, and conservative in social and political matters." Humphreys also brings women into his analysis by describing one of the female clients in his practice as a therapist who was arrested several years earlier for attempted arson at an abortion clinic. According to Humphreys she was deeply ambivalent about her own children and divorced after four years of a sexless marriage. Laud also discusses the activities of a right-wing Christian youth group that engaged in hate crimes and was led by a convicted sex offender.

Chapter 7. When Model Citizens Kill

Only three pages of this chapter were completed. The My Lai massacre in Vietnam is mentioned, and the many lynchings by the Ku Klux Klan are also briefly discussed. The mass murder during the Nazi Holocaust and the millions executed by Soviet Premier Joseph Stalin are also cited.

Other serial killers rely on two factors to maintain their cover: (1) a breastplate of righteousness, and (2) the social anonymity of their victims as runaways, derelicts, and street people. These examples illustrate the general point that "even mass murder—'multiple homicide' in the technical jargon of the law—is not a unitary phenomenon."

Chapter 8. Ayatollahs on the Left and Right

There is only an outline of chapter 8: Abstinence and the Assassins, Justice under Puritans, Righteousness and Rev. Jones, Sex and Mass Suicide, Massacres and Self-Hatred, A Question of Religion. The title of this chapter suggests that Humphreys was finally ready to discuss sexual deviance among liberal moral crusaders. He was also primed to attack celibacy as a dangerous avenue toward violence (long before the pedophilia scandals in the Roman Catholic Church), having earlier mentioned FBI Director J. Edgar Hoover as one such example.

Chapter 9. What's to Be Done?

As in chapter 8 there is also only an outline of chapter 9: How to Spot Moral Crusaders, Thinking Critically, Therapy as Defense, Finding the Moral Conservatives in Ourselves, Self-Protection from the Righteous Ones. According to the line of reasoning in this manuscript it should be easy to spot moral crusaders by focusing only on political conservatives. At this point in his life Humphreys was beginning to consider himself as much a therapist as a sociologist; thus in this chapter he was apparently planning to explain how therapy could be used to avoid these problems.

It may not be totally fair to be too harsh in criticizing this manuscript since it was not completed. As it stands, however, it is a rambling character assassination of conservative leaders caught in the act of sexual deviance. The empathy and compassion Humphreys exhibited in *Tearoom Trade* for those who wore the "breastplate of righteousness" is not found here. There is no theoretical integration in these presentations; thus Laud misses an opportunity for a possible expansion of the concept of the "breastplate of righteousness" to cover conservative crusaders. In its present form this manuscript is far from publishable quality, at least by any scholarly journal or university press. In any event, Humphreys forwarded the partially completed manuscript to his agent in July 1980 and projected completion in October of that year. He noted: "Due to the controversial subject matter, [the book] would benefit from legal counsel" (Humphreys 1980a). His agent dutifully sent the work to Simon and Schuster and to G. P. Putnam's Sons. The editor of the first publisher noted that, "it is not really written as a trade book for intelligent, sophisticated adults. . . . If it is the thesis of this book that many moral crusaders are sinners in sheep's clothing, then it is not very surprising" (Hills 1980). The editor at Putnam's agreed that "the catch-all survey approach is off-putting" (Amburn 1980).

Leaving Sociology

Part-time Sociologist: Working as a Psychotherapist

Humphreys had a private marriage and family counseling practice in Los Angeles from 1980 to 1988. He practiced primarily at night and on weekends. His counseling hours peaked shortly after he obtained his license, but they declined somewhat over the years. "Laud got an MFCC (marriage and family counseling credential). He could practice with that license in combination with his Ph.D. in sociology and about 3,000 hours of supervised counseling under a registered therapist. He and Brian both 'interned' with a gay therapist in L.A. Laud was able to count some of his pastoral counseling towards that requirement" (Lynch 2001a). "This was another way Laud hoped to make more money" (Miller 2001b).

After 1980 Laud published just two papers—one with Glenn Goodwin in 1982 and one with Anthony Russo in 1983 (Goodwin and Humphreys 1982; Russo and Humphreys 1983). In 1982 Brian Miller noted: "Currently, his main interest surrounds his psychotherapy practice in West Hollywood. His patients include, among others, tearoom people trying to develop positive gay identities. . . . [Laud was quoted as follows:] 'A large proportion of tearoom habitués I see in my practice experience impotence or premature ejaculation when they try to have sex outside tearooms. Interestingly, tearoom people report no lasting satisfaction from their encounters. They can have a dozen tearoom quickies in a week and still be horny'" (Miller 1982, 39).

Humphreys continued, discussing his new career as a therapist: "Remember, tearoom people don't so much come out of the closet as have the closet involuntarily ripped from around them. Such unanticipated exposure is devastating. My tearoom clients invariably have problems with depression. As a psychotherapist, I help these men rebuild their lives. My therapy is pragmatic too. I urge my tearoom clients to hire lawyers who have experience with tearoom cases and to fight the charges. . . . I also advise tearoom participants to try baths or [private] glory hole clubs [with wall openings for impersonal sex] as alternatives. While their context is similar to tearooms, they are safer and more conducive to developing gay pride. Higher self-esteem, including increased pride in being gay, will do more to control tearoom sex and help participants than all the deceptive resources police can muster" (Miller 1982, 40).

In 1981 Humphreys was "chastised by his sociology department at Pitzer for his lax teaching performance and too much time away from school" (Miller 2001b). He suffered from insomnia and was "very conflicted about the church. He loves the rituals and chants [as one would expect of anyone taking William Laud's name], but he hates the church as the primary oppressor of gays." In April Laud's five-year evaluation made it abundantly clear that his teaching, advising, committee work, and other professional performance had slipped badly. He was routinely late to class and was not available outside the classroom to students (Pitzer 1981). The tone of this letter indicates that this substandard performance had been going on for some years, perhaps shortly after he was promoted to full professor in 1975. Existing records for 1985 indicate that Humphreys wrote to the acting dean of the faculty (Humphreys 1985): "I have attended an AA meeting, have conferred at length with two fellow psychotherapists (one a psychiatrist and the other a clinical psychologist) who are recovering alcoholics, and have spent a sleepless night trying to deal with my conflicts. This letter is the result, therefore, of some obsession and an honest attempt to maintain my sanity and sobriety."

In this letter, for some unknown reason, he describes his conflict with Alvin Gouldner (Humphreys 1985): "That conflict resulted in my hospitalization with a concussion and broken ribs, his loss of the honorary title of Max Weber Distinguished Professor of Social Theory, my loss of a teaching contract and a million dollar research grant, the resignation of ten professors from the Sociology Department, and the crippling of that Department." Here Humphreys's grasp of his personal history seems to be slipping, or at least exaggerated. There is no evidence that Laud lost, or applied for, a million-dollar grant, although Rainwater applied for a large research grant. While several professors were upset, there is no indication that any professors resigned because Humphreys was assaulted. Yancy (2001b) indicated that, "the suggestion that Laud suffered broken ribs and a concussion from the 'altercation' with Al is news to me. I saw Laud soon after it occurred, in fact participated in his dissertation defense, and have no recollection of his having any noticeable physical injury. It is the case Gouldner's title was temporarily suspended, but this had little to do with Laud, but a great deal to do with the destructive nature of Al and his relationships in the department." According to Rainwater (2001), "As best I can remember Laud did not bring suit. He talked to the police but their view was that since there were no witnesses there was nothing they could do. We also guessed that the university had told them to keep it quiet. Later, when I moved to Harvard and he to Albany we continued to work together. He spent time doing fieldwork in the Boston gay scene, which was the beginning of his study of gay liberation. I saw him last some years later when he was in Cambridge for a conference and came to dinner, chipper as ever and telling us about his life in California."

Leaving Brian

Humphreys's relationship with Miller ended in October 1983. Laud then lived alone until his death. He told Fred Lynch (2001a) a year or two prior to his death that "relationships suck." "He became very active in AA and that consumed a lot of time and energy." Many friends recalled that there was continuing bad blood between Laud and Brian that survived even after Laud's death. "In September 1983 Laud begins to attend AA meetings" (Miller 2001a).

For his part Brian recalled these years in this way (Miller 2001b): "The divorce from Nancy caused Laud to have severe money problems since he now maintained two separate households and was paying child support. In spite of this, Laud was very generous and would often spend money that he didn't have. In addition, alcoholism and other mental problems began to take hold of Laud. Thus, the last ten years of his life were not so good." There is no doubt that Laud's "alcoholism and other mental problems" could account for the precipitous decline in the quality of his writing and teaching, and in the maintenance of his commitments to others. Carrier (2001) remembered that, "Laud lost much of the zest, intellectual and moral capacity that he had once so boldly demonstrated. On the other hand, near the end of Laud's life Nancy and Laud became friends again and her eyesight had been largely restored through laser surgery. At this point Laud also reconciled with the Episcopal Church, serving St. Thomas church in Hollywood."

Brian (Miller 2001a) emphasized the instrumental character of their relationship: "Our original deal is no longer useful to either of us. I don't need help with my sociology career since I've decided to switch to a career in psychotherapy. . . . Laud doesn't need my help to become accepted by the gay community because he's decided it is ageist and looksist and filled with substance abusers whom he doesn't want to be near." Of course, distinctions on the basis of age and physical beauty run deep among heterosexuals as well.

Humphreys retired from teaching in December 1986, and Pitzer had a going-away party for him. A video tape was made of Laud Humphreys's farewell party that has been retained by the Pitzer College Archives. The video reveals that Laud was missing most of his hair, which he explained was the result of chemotherapy and radiation treatment for his recently diagnosed and aggressive lung cancer. He conceded that because of his divorce and the consequent need for extra money he had become a therapist. This new career caused him to be less and less involved with Pitzer and hastened his retirement. He also admitted that he had been an alcoholic during most of his tenure at Pitzer, having only joined Alcoholics Anonymous and become sober in 1983. These confessions were mixed with self-promotion. Humphreys reminded the small audience that he had been awarded tenure at SUNY–Albany in 1972 but nevertheless had resigned to take the position at Pitzer. He also recalled that he had decided as well against pursuing the chance for a position at the University of Southern California at that time. And, ever on the attack, he criticized the Rev. Jimmy Swaggart and Republican Senator Joseph McCarthy as prime examples of crusading moral conservatives that in reality were sexual deviants as he proclaimed that his major theoretical contribution was the notion of the "breastplate of righteousness."

Death soon followed at the early age of fifty-seven, on August 23, 1988, from smoking-related lung cancer (*Claremont Courier* 1988, 12): "Known, by self-admission as a professor, a priest, an author, an anti-Vietnam war activist." Such a death was not a surprise to Laud's friends and associates since, as Henslin recalled from graduate school, it was known that Humphreys "couldn't sleep an entire night without waking up several times to smoke" (Henslin 2001b).

7

The Legacy of Laud

Politics, Substance, and Professional Ethics

A Short Life: Theologian, Scholar, and Activist, Father and Friend

Laud Humphreys's life was always tumultuous, fast-paced, and full of risk-taking behavior, including his chain-smoking addiction and alcohol abuse. One could say he was also a risk taker of a different kind in his sociology, his activism, his teaching, and his preaching. After completing seminary training he was a priest for approximately ten years and was in constant trouble with both parishioners and clerics alike. In the early 1960s he was forced out of his parish in Oklahoma and was fired again from his church post in Wichita in 1965. He was in graduate school from 1965 to 1968, and during this stint he was physically assaulted by one of his professors. He was arrested for an antiwar protest in 1970, terrorized by law enforcement authorities and local citizens, and then jailed in 1972. He came out in 1974, left his wife, Nancy, and the children, obtaining a divorce in 1978, and then left Brian Miller in 1983, essentially leaving the field of sociology in 1980. In 1988 he was dead at age fifty-seven. He was a graduate student for a mere three years. He was an assistant professor at Southern Illinois University–Edwardsville for nearly two years until he was forced to flee the community. He had been an associate professor for two years at SUNY–Albany and had left that faculty, perhaps after a confrontation with a senior colleague. Then he was an associate professor at Pitzer for three years, from 1972 to 1975 and a professor beginning in 1975, and then he became a therapist in 1980. Probably soon after 1975 his performance as a sociologist had slipped dramatically. Humphreys was constantly on the move, almost seeming to be running away from himself. He was always leaving. He left the priesthood, he left SIU, he left SUNY-Albany, he left Nancy, he left Brian, and he also left sociology and Pitzer College.

There is no doubt that Humphreys's antiracist positions as a member of the clergy, his antiwar activism at Washington University, his flouting of his newfound gay identity, and his unusually assertive style of writing and research are all linked together. It is not merely that Humphreys was ahead of his time—and indeed he was—but that, although most sociologists of his generation opposed racism and the Vietnam War, they did so quietly, perhaps merely making some passing comments in class or over cocktails. Maintaining the myth of objectivity was, and remains, important to most sociologists. On the other hand, Laud felt obliged to carry every position to its logical extreme. Anything less, in his view, was cowardly.

A complete picture of Laud Humphreys must note that, although he was ever vigilant in broadcasting the unethical treatment of gay men, in other facets of his life he was not so reflective about moral issues. By all accounts, he had deserted a faithful, loving, and supportive wife to live with Brian Miller. Not only was his wife blind at the time and suffering from diabetes, but she also was left with two young children to rear alone. Money had always been in short supply in the Humphreys household, and this was especially true after the couple divorced. Nancy and the children were forced to move from their suburban home into a condominium. Clearly Laud felt strongly that, to be true to himself, he had to leave. His decision in this regard is most revealing about his life, in that he seemed always to place himself at the center of every choice he made. Another example of his self-involvement is in his resolve to conduct a public antiwar protest at the Illinois draft board offices. The protest may also be said to have centered on him, as he had made the decision to become involved without consulting his wife and children.

Henslin (2001b) recalled that Humphreys was at once "fearless, outgoing, outspoken, self-centered and conceited. He loved an audience, [and] he liked to shock people with mentioning salacious sexual details." Throughout his life and career Humphreys raised thorny ethical questions. In 1971 he wrote to Professor Lewis Coser, chair of the ASA Committee on Professional Ethics, posing a tough question. He asked for advice on what to do with stolen FBI records that had come into his possession (Humphreys 1971b). He told Coser: "I did not steal the documents nor do I know who did. The data for my research are not stolen property, but they are reproductions of stolen property." He then asked: "Who, indeed, are the 'research subjects' in a study of social control agencies: agency personnel, the Director, legislators who establish and finance an agency, or those who elect the legislators? If we reply that the scientist must not be an adversary, I think we must dismiss such persons as Karl Marx, Pasteur, Salk, and C. Wright Mills from the rolls of science." There is no evidence in Humphreys's files that Coser replied, even though he had earlier expressed concern about covert research in a letter to the editor of *American Sociological Review (ASR)*. Coser (1959) had condemned a covert participant observation study of enlisted men engaged in U.S. Air Force basic training, published in *ASR* (Sullivan et al. 1958).

Theory and Biography

As a pioneer in his being a publicly gay sociologist, Humphreys's sexual behavior was undoubtedly considered unprofessional and immoral by many. Moreover, he had the ongoing capacity to carry every moral value to its extreme. Good ideas, from his perspective, were often seen as bad ideas. As a priest his sermons bludgeoned parishioners with the need to attend to society's outcasts. The norm of academic freedom, in his hands while he was a graduate student, became a vehicle for his harassment of a distinguished senior faculty member. If others such as Liebow (1967) in *Tally's Corner* could use fieldwork to study the poor on the streets, then Humphreys, in his view, could observe men performing oral sex in restrooms.

His behavior in the classroom could also be extreme, as was his demeanor in the Pitzer sociology department. He also pushed moral boundaries in the community. These were all aspects of his deviance. Humphreys eagerly engaged in same-sex dating and dancing at faculty parties and appears to have been the first sociologist to come out—in his case in the most public of forums, at the meetings of the ASA. By eagerly leading student demonstrations against the war in Vietnam, by writing for the gay press and delighting in damning political leaders in print, Humphreys also pushed the moral boundaries of academia.

Laud provided a clear vision of the role punishment plays in higher education. He was initially punished at Washington University where his research, his activism, and his personal conflict with Alvin Gouldner were targeted as boundary transgressions. His research focusing on fellatio was reason enough to imagine that he would be condemned. Even fieldwork on heterosexual fellatio would be devalued, as would a detailed description of heterosexual intercourse. In addition, his research in public restrooms could be seen as intruding into the lives of others. Aiding and abetting this sexual behavior by warning of approaching law enforcement was technically criminal activity.

Government officials considered Humphreys a political radical. To this we can add that at least some of his colleagues who served as government informants obviously agreed with this assessment. At the very least his carrying issues to the extreme was undoubtedly considered unwise by most of his colleagues. Serving jail time clearly is highly unusual for university professors. Most individuals with this characteristic as a part of their biography are excluded from posts in higher education. A public audience gave Humphreys a visibility that made him a likely target for government punishment. At times he seemed oblivious or indifferent to the risks he was taking in routinely intruding beyond the moral boundaries of his social groups. Most important, even today Humphreys is routinely condemned in sociology textbooks and held up as a negative role model for how *not* to practice sociology.

It is instructive to compare the treatment Humphreys was given to that received by sociologist Charles Moskos of Northwestern University. At its annual meetings in Toronto in 1997 the American Sociological Association gave Moskos an award for "work that increases understanding of sociology outside of academe" (Basinger 1997). Among Moskos's other activities had been work with the Clinton administration in developing the "don't ask, don't tell" policy on homosexuals in the military. A group of gay and lesbian members of the ASA publicly protested this award, since they alleged that this policy had done considerable harm to gay people in the military.

Humphreys noted in his 1972 textbook that homosexuals in the military risked immediate discharge if their sexual orientation became public. Thus individual members of the armed services cannot complain of being abused on the basis of their sexual orientation. This requirement of secrecy set the stage for routine humiliations, beatings, and even murder of gay men in the military (*Washington Post* 1999). Nonetheless Moskos was rewarded by the ASA for his service to government, even while damaging the interests of gay and lesbian people, whereas Humphreys has been condemned even while arguably serving to normalize homosexuals. Just as Durkheim (1964) explained it, the punishment of specific deviant behavior provides rich testimony on the moral and intellectual boundaries of the group, in this case the discipline of sociology and higher education in general.

Clearly the life of Laud Humphreys was filled with frustration. He failed to see any end to the U.S. war machine in spite of his extreme commitment to nonviolence. He also failed to see an end to widespread gay bashing or the achievement of real equality for gays and lesbians in American society. Indeed, as one early reviewer commented, it is possible to see "Humphreys as an exemplary figure who succeeded, as it were, by his failure" (Koffler 2003). Koffler (2003) also noted that in Laud's life "there were scandals galore, protest and movement stories, but this is not a heroic moment for such a work" as his biography. We disagree. It is hard to know when an optimal time for Laud's biography might be in a nation almost continually making war.

Covert Research and Checking for Honesty and Reliability

Assessing the honesty and reliability of Laud's data is difficult. That he finished all the course requirements and his dissertation in precisely three years is certainly remarkable. We must remember, too, that he did not allow even his dissertation supervisor to see the notes from his fieldwork. Thus it is possible that he could have fabricated data or, more likely, embellished on the truth to make patterns more dramatic or apparent. However, a careful review of his papers stored in the One Institute and Archives in Los Angeles makes this seem highly unlikely. These papers contain many copies of a "Systematic Observation Sheet" (See Appendix D), and these forms were filled out in considerable detail. Had Laud intended to mislead, such detail would have been unnecessary.

The Breastplate of Righteousness

Humphreys's findings regarding the perfectly upright and conservative self-presentations of his tearoom subjects are reflected in more recent research. His notion that "hidden deviants" will wear a "breastplate of righteousness" and portray an image of superpropriety to mask their deviance is widely applicable to the sociology of deviance and to the sociology of identity in general. Schacht (2001) reports on his being terminated at the Jesuit Gonzaga University for his research on gay drag queens. "Often donning brilliantly embroidered gowns, especially for special occasions, the priests were seen as the pious icons and rightful leaders of the university"; one of the ways they showed their piety was to express intolerance for research among gays, drag queens, and other stigmatized gender and sexual "deviants." Brekhus (2003) found that some suburban gays used a similar presentation of superpropriety to minimize their stigma and oppression. Brekhus implies that the concept may be generally applicable to members of other oppressed groups as well. For example, some immigrants may present themselves as righteously "American" to an extreme, and some members of criminal subcultures may present themselves as pious and beyond fault in other areas of their lives. Moreover, Humphreys's own work as a member of the clergy, his marriage to a beautiful woman, and the adoption of children all reflect an attempt to take on the "breastplate of righteousness," similar to his father's efforts.

The Ethical Maxim: Do No Harm (Considering Medicine and Psychology)

One wonders if the sexual orientation of Laud Humphreys makes a difference in judging his research ethically and empirically. Since it is now known that he was gay, his research strategy seems somewhat less prying and invasive then when it was assumed (as textbooks still imply) that he was heterosexual. He was not so much an intruding outsider as he was an insider striving to learn more about a subculture of which he was a part. As with ethnic and racial minority scholars who study their own ethnicity or minority group, having some insider knowledge and insider access to members of the same oppressed group may be seen as the ethnographic advantage of studying one's own kind.

Humphreys's substantive findings that many individuals who practice homosexuality are non-stereotypical and may even have a "heterosexual identity" and live a "heterosexual lifestyle" are now routinely accepted. There is currently a burgeoning literature dealing with stereotypes imposed on gay men and lesbian women. Humphreys's work in showing that publicly pious heterosexuals could be privately deviant "commuters" to a "part-time homosexual sexual identity" (Brekhus 2003) was an early pioneering work in the normalizing of homosexuality. The impact of Laud's work has been profound. Now people feel free to come out, and do so more and more. As this behavior becomes more common, it serves to normalize these people and their behavior. During Laud's life, and indeed during his sociological career, there were significant political gains for the gay and lesbian community. This progress includes the fact that coming out is now a routine occurrence in the academy, a trail Humphreys clearly helped to blaze.

David Pittman (2001) has argued that, to be fair, "Laud's dissertation and the subsequent book, *Tearoom Trade,* must be understood in the social context of the time when it was initiated and completed. First, the status of gay and lesbian people was quite different than currently. Furthermore, homosexuality was a taboo topic. Washington University in the late 1960s was similar to other American universities in that there were so far as I know no openly gay and lesbian faculty members. There was no non-discrimination policy in reference to gays and lesbians and, of course, domestic partnership benefits were unknown. There are all three of the above at Washington University today. Thus Laud was a pioneer in research in gay studies despite the numerous criticisms that may be leveled against his study in social science research courses." It is clear that Laud could not have been open about his sexual preference at the time and felt he could not share information on his sample and field notes, even with his faculty advisers. Pittman continued: "I will leave it to others to explore the interaction of Laud's biography with his choice of a research topic. Was his research study a means by which he was coping with questions of his sexual identity at the time? Those who wish to examine Laud's research must analyze this question of sexual identity to fully understand the scholar and researcher."

Even considering the gains of the lesbian and gay communities and gay and lesbian researchers, it is arguable that there have been some losses to the discipline to institutional power wielded through university Institutional Review Boards (IRBs) created to protect the interests of human subjects used in research. Much of the increased control on research is a consequence of the abuses of medical researchers. The infamous 1930s Tuskegee Syphilis Experiment clearly played some role here (U.S. Department of Health, Education, and Welfare 1973; Jones 1993). In this study begun in 1932 in Macon County, Alabama, 399 African American men who had been diagnosed with syphilis in its final phase were studied over several decades to determine the progress of the disease if left untreated. The men were routinely examined, and autopsies conducted, but none of the men were told of their disease, and none were treated. The subjects were coaxed into participation by being offered a guarantee of burial stipends for their families.

Psychology also played some role in the development of IRB restrictions. The Milgram studies on obedience (1974), where subjects were instructed to administer what they believed to be electric shocks, are often cited as a significant abuse even though it is unclear that any research subject was actually harmed. The most that can be said is that perhaps some subjects were dismayed at their own behavior. The Zimbardo

(1972) study of a mock prison may well have had more of a significant impact on subjects, especially as those randomly selected to play the role of the "guards" became aware of their own capacity to abuse other subjects assigned the role of "prisoners."

We should note here that psychologists have also studied social interaction in toilets, with a not unexpected quantitative twist. Middlemist and his colleagues (1976) studied the relationship between urination time, urination persistence, and the distance to the next nearest person in the toilet. These researchers found highly statistically significant differences in that the closer the human contact, the longer the urination took to be completed, and the less persistent was the urination stream. The authors concluded that invasions of personal space cause discomfort.

Even more outrageous was the research of Putney and Cadwallader (1957, 40) involving the following deception: "a tape recording was played through a radio at a social gathering of eleven individuals. Four of these were observers. The recording contained seven 'newscasts,' . . . which reported a new international crisis, an air raid alert, and the outbreak of an atomic war. . . . A second machine recorded the group responses." The experiment lasted thirty minutes. It took place in November 1953 at the height of the Cold War, making these developments seem credible. A final announcement on the radio reported bombing in a nearby city whereupon it was announced that broadcasting would cease. One person began to sob, but most merely held one another. Once the deception was announced there was "shouting, crying, and laughing [as well as] hysterical crying" (43). Many subjects understandably expressed anger at the experimenters. "The effects on some individuals continued for a few weeks, and in one case for several months" (43). In their own defense the experimenters argued that "there is no question of the importance of understanding the nature and causes of panic interaction" and that "we must avoid closing off vital areas of research" (43–44).

Putney and Cadwallader approvingly cited French's (1944) study of groups of undergraduates subjected to fear. Here there were six students in each group. After these groups completed a problem-solving session, the experimenter left the group, locking the students in the room from the outside. Thick smoke was soon pumped into the room at a rapid rate and a fire engine siren was used to simulate the sound of a fire engine on the street outside the building. In many of the groups the experiment was so convincing that group members attempted to break down the door.

In a deception directly related to homosexuality Bramel's research (1962) to test cognitive dissonance theory involved subjects who were told that they had homosexual tendencies. Bramel writes: "Imagine, for example, a person who considers homosexuality a bad and disgusting thing; on some occasion he is suddenly exposed to information strongly implying that he has homosexual tendencies" (121). All subjects were falsely informed that measures of psychogalvanic skin response would indicate their homosexual arousal when presented pictures of men. In reality, the experimenter controlled the measurements.

Sociology: Caught in the Net

Contrary to Krisberg's concerns noted by Humphreys (1975, 225), one is hard-pressed to see in the studies of sociologists Becker, Polsky, Goffman, Liebow any abuse of human subjects. Polsky studied the tactics of pool hustlers using participant observation. Becker studied marihuana users using interviews and dance band musicians through participant observation. Liebow used participant observation to study homeless black men in Washington, D.C. Even without a clear record of abuses in his discipline, sociologist Donald Warwick (1975b, 106) demanded that, "government must step in and prevent the most flagrant abuses, especially public deception." Sociologist Paul Davidson Reynolds (1983) expressed deep antagonism at criticism of IRBs. Krisberg's criticism of Becker, Polsky, Liebow, and Goffman, none of which used informed consent, was prophetic, for it is arguable that IRBs might not approve any of these seminal studies of human behavior. All of these studies involved some level of deception, and none of the researchers received the kinds of written informed consent that is now almost always required before one can conduct observations or interviews.

Horowitz and Rainwater (1975) predicted a "tame sociology," and indeed this is precisely what has happened. It is arguable that it is no longer possible to study hospitalized psychiatric patients, marihuana smokers, homeless black men, or pool hustlers without first distributing and getting signatures on informed-consent forms. Collecting signed forms generally is not possible with those who are being observed, since they will initially distrust outsiders. Most ethnographers establish trust only through gaining rapport, and thus a consent form presented at the outset usually will have the effect of severing ties before trust can begin to be cultivated. The power of government now shields us from knowing the truth about ghettos, tearooms, marihuana users, and abuses of patients in psychiatric hospitals. Certainly it is no longer possible to conduct research like the Milgram obedience study or the Zimbardo simulated prison study. The studies of Milgram and Zimbardo are classics, at least in part, because they can no longer be conducted.

It is interesting to speculate on patterns of IRB response to some other classic studies. Beginning in 1930 LaPiere (1934) traveled widely in the United States with a Chinese couple. After stopping at more than two hundred hotels and restaurants they were refused service on only one occasion. Yet when contacted later, the response from over 90 percent of these establishments indicated that they would not accommodate Chinese patrons. There is no evidence that any thought was given to informed consent. Lindesmith's (1947) fieldwork among opiate addicts might also arouse IRB concern, as would the Chambliss (1978) study of those involved in organized crime. Neither utilized informed consent. The Schwartz and Skolnick (1962) study of actual patterns of employment discrimination was also conducted without prior consent from employers, as was the Tittle and Rowe (1973) study of cheating by students when grading their prescored tests.

Others have argued that, "according to these [IRB] guidelines, Humphreys never could have researched or written *Tearoom Trade*. In fact, these criteria fundamentally outlaw data gathered through direct observation or observation on nearly all aspects of deviant behavior" (Denzin and Lincoln 1994, 389). As we have seen, Krisberg, Warwick, Glazer, Daniels, and Reynolds ganged up on Laud's study. The claim still stands (Galliher 1973, 97): "Ironically it is sociologists themselves who have helped politicize their craft by treating methodological and empirical problems of data collection as political and ethical questions."

Rik Scarce was jailed for 159 days for contempt of court for his failure to obey a court order to release the names of his informants (1995) who had described to him their destruction of university property during the liberation of research animals. Scarce (1995, 88) noted that the ASA Code of Ethics speaks to the issue very clearly: "Confidential information provided by research participants must be treated as such by sociologists, even when this information enjoys no legal protection or privilege and legal force is applied." Accordingly, the ASA initially supported Scare's refusal to release his informants' names, but after an appeals court rejected his position the organization quickly reversed itself. Years later Scarce observed that the ASA has since abandoned this tenet of its ethical code: "The ASA's ethical stance requires that the researcher inform on research subjects" (2001). On the other hand, Richard Leo obeyed a court order to testify about his confidential research data, and thus avoided both jail and the need for any false assurances from the ASA leadership. Conducting fieldwork in a police station, Leo (1995) had passed himself off as a supporter of the necessity of questionable interrogation tactics of police officers.

Van den Hoonard (2001) has found evidence of a moral panic in university human subjects' research guidelines. The hazards created by social science research are routinely exaggerated, using *Tearoom Trade* as a prime example. Such regulations make qualitative fieldwork especially difficult since the precise list of questions to be posed to respondents cannot be known in advance. Thus interview schedules cannot be shown to IRBs. Demanding that field-workers obtain written consent forms would preclude most ethnographic observation of natural social interaction. Hollister (2002, 253) persuasively argues that, "Institutional Review Board regulations assume medical research using controlled experiments. This model is inappropriate for qualitative research, especially for field studies, for they cannot be designed in advance. Rather, the procedures and entire research design must be flexible enough to be changed as researchers become more familiar with the field site." In addition to the impediments to all qualitative fieldwork, Hollister (2002, 254) also notes that IRBs make research on sexual behavior especially difficult. "Human subjects' regulations have likely had a chilling effect on the sociology of sexuality. [The Humphreys ethnography was] conducted prior to their imposition, while throughout the 80s and 90s initiative on social scientific thinking on sexuality has been taken up by the humanities, who analyze texts rather than human situations. The consequence is the shortage of sociological research that could guide policymaking on AIDS." This helps to explain the uneven development of queer theory across the humanities and the social sciences, as well as the continuing ignorance surrounding public policy and the AIDS epidemic.

The upshot of this is that sociologists find it much more difficult to study human behavior, and often merely investigate what people say about their behavior. This is highly limiting and misleading (Blumer 1955; Deutscher 1966, 1973). One need only remember Humphreys's concept of the "breastplate of righteousness" to know that surface attitudes do not necessarily correlate with actual behavior. Blumer (1955, 61) claimed: "Attitudes do not provide the first line of proof. The overwhelming proportion of attitude studies do not even attempt to concern themselves with action. . . . Accordingly, they tell us nothing of the relation of attitude to action . . . against the idea that the tendency or attitude controls the act is the effect of the activities of others on one's own activity." In other words, human behavior is dynamic and a product of social interaction, not predetermined by individual attitudes. Deutscher (1966) has also argued that social scientists should study behavior rather than what people say about their behavior. We need to study the process involved in human behavior that analysis of quantitative variables does not allow (Deutscher 1973), especially if we are to maintain an exciting, innovative and progressive discipline such as envisioned by Laud Humphreys.

Having said all this it is still true that some privacy is necessary in a good and just society. It is also true that social scientists still are in the process of deciding what ethical standards should apply to their craft (Jaarsma 2002; Kancelbaum 2002). At a minimum, a good society affords people some privacy in places such as public restrooms and private homes. Laud's research could have caused his subjects great harm. He could have released the names of the politically conservative men he first encountered in the tearooms. This might well have resulted in ruined lives and even suicides. Although Humphreys handled his data with great care, some question whether a decision of such importance should be left entirely to the discretion of the researcher. Even so, Laud Humphreys's research makes important contributions to our discipline and to our lives. The fact that general ethical principles and Laud Humphreys's research are difficult to reconcile is what makes him such an interesting case.

Epilogue

There is no doubt that had Laud Humphreys not shortened his life by smoking cigarettes, Americans would be hearing from him today. It was recently noted that, in spite of the growing acceptance of homosexuality, in the new millennium tearooms and "cruising networks still generally resemble [what] Humphreys studied a generation ago" (Hoover 2003, A31). And even though "many colleges now provide more social outlets for gay students does not mean that tearooms have lost their appeal" (A31). Tearooms still provide an outlet for those who fear identification with a gay subculture. In 2001 the Boston University Police Department began undercover stings arresting many men in the campus bathrooms. George Washington University also uses plainclothes officers to patrol bathrooms. It is safe to assume that Laud would protest such law-enforcement practices.

As the AIDS epidemic has ravaged the world, he would certainly be a champion of increased spending on AIDS research and treatment. And as an academic he would be among those insisting that all universities offer complete spousal benefits for those involved in same-sex relationships. And without doubt Laud would have a leadership role among those criticizing university IRBs as they have moved to circumscribe social science research. Surely Laud would have a public role in the contemporary peace movement. This said, it is clear how much American sociology and American society miss by his absence. Just now, Laud would be proud of the Episcopal church for the ordination of its first openly gay bishop.

Appendixes

References

Index

Appendix A
Laud Humphreys's Vita

2/83

Curriculum Vita

Laud Humphreys

Office

Pitzer College
Claremont, CA 91711
(714) 621-9000, ext. 3067
Secretary: ext. 3155

Residence

2403 Earl Street
Los Angeles, CA 90039
(213) 660-4485

Education

Graduate, Chickasha (Oklahoma) High School, 1948
B.A., Colorado College, Colorado Springs, CO, 1952
M. Div., Seabury-Western Theological Seminary, Evanston, IL, 1955
Ph.D., Washington University, St. Louis, MO, 1968

Honors

Poetry Prize, Colorado College, 1952
NIMH Pre-Doctoral Research Fellowships, 1966-67, 1967-68
C. WRIGHT MILLS AWARD of the Society for the Study of Social Problems,
1970 (for the outstanding book on a critical social issue)

Academic Employment

RESEARCH ASSISTANT, Medical Care Research Center, St. Louis, MO, 1965-66
RESEARCH ASSOCIATE, Medical Care Research Center, St. Louis, MO, 1967-68
LECTURER IN SOCIOLOGY, Washington University, St. Louis, MO 1967-68
ASSISTANT PROFESSOR OF SOCIOLOGY, Southern Illinois University,
Edwardsville, IL, 1968-70
ASSOCIATE PROFESSOR, School of Criminal Justice, Statue University of
New York, Albany, 1970-72
ASSOCIATE PROFESSOR OF SOCIOLOGY, Pitzer College, Claremont, CA, 1972-75

CURRENT

PROFESSOR OF SOCIOLOGY, Pitzer College, Claremont, CA, 1975-
PROFESSOR OF CRIMINAL JUSTICE, Claremont Graduate School, Claremont, CA,
1980-
CALIFORNIA LICENSED PSYCHOTHERAPIST, M.F.C.C. License #M14712, private
counseling practice in Los Angeles, 1980-

Professional Organizations

American Sociological Association
Society for the Study of Social Problems
Pacific Sociological Association
International Academy of Sex Research (Charter Member)
Academy of Criminal Justice Sciences

Humphreys - 2

Board Memberships and Elected Offices

EDITORIAL BOARD, Archives of Sexual Behavior, 1970-77, 1981-
EDITORIAL BOARD, Journal of Homosexuality, 1973-81
PRESIDENT, BOARD OF DIRECTORS, Institute for the Study of Human
    Resources, 1973-83
ELECTED MEMBER, Council of the Sex Roles Section, American Sociological
    Association, 1973-75
ELECTED MEMBER, Faculty Senate of the Claremont Colleges, 1973-76
CHAIR, Research and Development Committee, Pitzer College, 1974-76
    (Member, 1980-81); Admissions and Financial Aid Committee, 1981-83
CONVENER, Sociology Field Group, Pitzer College, 1974-76
CHAIR, Committee on Standards and Freedom of Research, Publication,
    and Teaching, Society for the Study of Social Problems, 1975-77
CHAIR, Task Force on Homosexuality and the Profession, Society for the
    Study of Social Problems, 1977-79
EDITORIAL BOARD, Alternative Lifestyles, 1977-
COUNCIL OF OVERSEERS, Mariposa Education and Research Foundation, 1979-
ELECTED CHAIR, Sexual Behavior Division, Society for the Study of
    Social Problems, 1979-81

Public Presentations

CHAIR AND ORGANIZER: Session on Deviant Behavior, ASA meetings,
Washington, DC, 1970; Section on Gender Roles, Pacific Sociological
Association, Spokane, WA, 1978.

INVITED SPEAKER: Sidore Lecture Series, University of New Hampshire,
1971; Symposium on Deviance, University of Minnesota, 1971; School
of Psychiatry, UCLA, 1972; Kansas University, 1973; Denver University
1973; University of Colorado, Boulder, 1973; Oklahoma University,
1974; Cal. State Univ., L.A., 1974; Occidental College, 1975, 1977;
Cal. State Univ., Northridge, 1976; University of Alberta, Edmonton,
Canada, 1976; University of California, San Diego, 1976; Cal. State
Univ., Long Beach, 1976; New York University, 1977; Cal. State Univ.,
Fullerton; Keynote Speaker, National Conference of the Gay
Academic Union, UCLA, 1980; Public Events Speaker, Oklahoma University,
1981; Banquet Speaker, Nebraska Sociological Symposium, University
of Nebraska, Lincoln, 1981.

PANELIST: "Communicating Sociology to the Public," meetings of the
Pacific Sociological Association, Scottsdale, AZ, 1973; "Third Sex,"
American Orthopsychiatric Association, San Francisco, 1974; "The New
Ambisexuality," Southern California Psychiatric Association, Century
City, 1974; "The Case of the Gay Corpse: Homosexual Victims of
Homicide," American Society of Criminology, Tucson, AZ, 1976; "Ethics
in Social Research," Pacific Sociological Association, San Francisco,
1980.

Humphreys - 3

Public Presentations (Continued)

CRITICAL DISCUSSANT: Section on "Theoretical Perspectives on Homo-
sexuality," meetings of the American Sociological Association,
Montreal, Canada, 1974; Section on "Homosexuality," American
Sociological Association, New York, 1976.

TELEVISION APPEARANCES: Interviewed with Melvin Belli on the Kennedy
Show, Ch. 7, Chicago, 1971
With Professors Irving Horowitz and John Howard, "Sociology
Today," Ch. 13, New York, 1971
Helped research and interviewed as expert on "The Saturday Show,"
KNBC, Ch. 4, Los Angeles, 1974
Debate with John Briggs on KCET, Ch. 28, Los Angeles , 1978
Interviewed on "Briggs Initiative" show with Dear Abby as host,
Ch. 7, KABC, Los Angeles, 1978
Interviewed by Paul Moyer on the "Sunday Show," KNBC, Ch 4, 1978
Interviewed on "Child Molestation" on "Vox Populi," KCOP, Ch 13,
1981

Teaching Experience

LECTURER IN SOCIOLOGY, Washington University, 1967-68: Soc. 205,
Introduction to Sociology; Soc. 312, Criminology; Soc. 325, Urban
Social Problems

ASSISTANT PROFESSOR OF SOCIOLOGY, Southern Illinois University, 1968-70:
Soc. 301, Principles of Sociology; Soc. 302, Contemporary Social
Problems; Soc. 372, Criminology; Soc. 405, Current Sociology; Soc. 472,
Treatment and Prevention of Crime; Soc. 474, Crime and the Legal
Process; Soc. 489, Probation, Classification, and Parole; Soc. 534,
Inter-Group Relations

ASSOCIATE PROFESSOR OF CRIMINAL JUSTICE, State University of New York
at Albany, 1970-72: CRJ 500, Pro-Seminar in the Nature of Crime
(with Hans Toch); CRJ 601, Crime, Deviation and Conformity (with
Hans Toch); CRJ 700, Public Order Crime; CRJ 788, Methods of Field
Observation

ASSOCIATE PROFESSOR/PROFESSOR OF SOCIOLOGY, Pitzer College, 1972- :
Soc. 1, Sociology and Its View of the World; Soc. 26, Introductory
Social Problems; Soc. 36, Sociology of Deviance; Soc. 102, Methods of
Field Research; Soc. 133, The Prison Experience; Soc. 137, Stigmatized
Sexual Behavior; Soc. 140, Social Sources of Violence; Soc. 158,
Subcultures and Occupations; Soc. 193, Crime in Mass Society

PROFESSOR OF CRIMINAL JUSTICE, Claremont Graduate School, 1975- :
Gov. 202, Qualitative Research Methods; Seminar on Crime and Delinquency
(NIMH Training Program); Gov. 358, Subcultures and Occupations

Humphreys - 4

Fields of Research and Special Interest

> Criminology, Violence, Stigmatized Behavior, Gender Roles,
> Homosexuality, Subcultures and Occupations, Qualitative Research
> Methods.

Research Experience

> From 1965-68, I worked with the Medical Care Research Center, St. Louis,
> MO. There I completed an exploratory study of a private medical
> practice and worked on the initial stages of a community health
> survey.

> During 1970-71, I served as a consultant for the Research Program in
> Family Behavior and Social Policy of the Harvard/M.I.T. Joint Center
> for Urban Studies, for the Laboratory in Community Mental Health of
> the Harvard Medical School, and the Institute of Juvenile Research
> of the State of Illinois.

> In the Summer of 1972, I was investigator of a National Science
> Foundation Project on the Nature of the Causes of Politicized Criminal
> identity in Prisons.

> From 1974-78, I served as principal evaluator for two major juvenile
> diversion projects in the San Gabriel Valley of Southern California.
> Here, I was concerned not only with the relative success of different
> treatment modalities in preventing recidivism but also with the
> general impact of the projects on the ten cities involved.

> Since 1974, I have been involved in a continuing study of homicides
> involving homosexual victims.

Books Published

> TEAROOM TRADE: IMPERSONAL SEX IN PUBLIC PLACES, Hawthorne, NY: Aldine,
> 1975 (expanded edition). Winner of the C. Wright Mills Award for
> the outstanding work on a critical social issue, 1970. Now in its
> fifth printing.

> The first edition of TEAROOM TRADE was published in 1970 by
> Aldine Publishing Co., then located in Chicago.

> A British edition, with a Foreward by D.J. West of Cambridge
> University, was published by Gerald Duckworth & Co. Ltd., of London
> in 1970. (Paperback, 1974).

> The German language edition, Klappen-Sexualitat, was published in
> paperback by Ferinand Enke Verlag of Stuffgart in 1974.

Humphreys - 5

<u>Books Published</u> (Continued)

The Revised Edition, with a "Retrospect on Ethical Issues," was published by Aldine in 1975 in both cloth and paper.

A second paperback edition was published by Aldine in 1978. Aldine has sold in excess of 30,000 copies, but there is no record of sales by the two foreign publishers.

Portions of the book have been reprinted in 14 different readers and texts.

OUT OF THE CLOSETS: THE SOCIOLOGY OF HOMOSEXUAL LIBERATION, Englewood Cliffs, NJ: Prentice-Hall, Inc., 1972. This is a Spectrum Book, published in both cloth and paperback. Now in its second printing.

<u>Articles Published</u>

"Crime and Criminology," in <u>The Encyclopedia Americana</u>, 1969 and subsequent editions.

"Mafia" and "Cosa Nostra." In <u>The Encyclopedia Americana</u>, 1969 and subsequent editions.

"Impersonal Sex in Public Places," in <u>Trans-action</u>, January 1970, pp. 10-25.

"New Styles in Homosexual Manliness," in <u>Trans-action</u>, March/April 1971, pp. 38-46, 64-65.

"Homosexual Exchanges in Public Places," pp. 129-142 in L. Rainwater (ed.), <u>Social Problems and Public Policy: Deviance and Liberty</u>. Hawthorne, NY: Aldine, 1974.

"Predicting the Unpredictable: Some Crime Prospects for the Decade," in <u>The Participant</u>, Winter, 1975.

"An Interview with Evelyn Hooker," in <u>Alternative Lifestyles: Changing Patterns in Marriage, Family & Intimacy</u>, Vol. 1, No. 2

"Being Odd Against All Odds," pp. 238-242 in R. Fedarico (ed.), <u>Sociology</u> (2nd edition). Reading, MA: Addison-Wesley, 1979.

"Exodus and Identity: The Emerging Gay Culture," pp. 134-147 in M. Levine (ed.), <u>Gay Men: The Sociology of Male Homosexuality</u>. New York: Harper and Row, 1979.

Humphreys - 6

Articles Published (Continued)

(with Brian Miller) "Identities in the Emerging Gay Culture,"
pp. 142-156 in J. Marmor (ed.), Homosexual Behavior: A Modern
Reappraisal. New York: Basic Books, 1980.

(with Brian Miller) "Keeping in Touch: Maintaining Contact with
Stigmatized Subjects," pp. 212-223 in W. Shaffir, R. Stebbins,
and A. Turowetz (eds.), Field Work Experience: Qualitative
Approaches to Social Research. New York: St. Martin's, 1980.

(with Brian Miller) "Lifestyles and Violence: Homosexual Victims
of Assault and Murder," pp. 169-185 in Qualitative Sociology, Vol. 3,
No. 3 (Fall), 1980.

(with Glenn Goodwin) "Freeze-Dried Stigma: Cybernetics and Social
Control," in Humanity and Society, Dec. 1982.

(with Anthony J. Russo) "Homosexuality and Crime," in Encyclopedia
of Crime and Justice, New York: Macmillan, 1983.

Major Book Reviews

The Discovery of the Asylum: Social Order and Disorder in the New
Republic by David J. Rothman, in Criminal Law Bulletin, September,
1971.

Three books on male prostitution, in Contemporary Sociology, January,
1978.

Homosexuality in Perspective by William H. Masters and Virginia E. Johnson,
in Society/Transaction, September, 1980.

Appendix B

Laud Humphreys's FBI File

FEDERAL BUREAU OF INVESTIGATION

FREEDOM OF INFORMATION/PRIVACY ACTS SECTION

COVER SHEET

SUBJECT

LAUD HUMPHREYS

aka: Robert Allan Laud Humphreys

NR002 SI PLAIN   TELETYPE

917 AM   URGENT   5-7-70 BLR

TO   DIRECTOR

FROM SPRINGFIELD (52-   ) 1P

ROBERT ALLAN LAUD HUMPHREYS; DGP; SSA.

   ON TUESDAY, MAY FIVE LAST, A LARGE GROUP OF STUDENTS
AND INSTRUCTORS, SOUTHERN ILLINOIS UNIVERSITY, EDWARDSVILLE,
ILLINOIS, ENTERED SELECTIVE SERVICE HEADQUARTERS OF LDB
ONE SIX FIVE-ONE SIX SEVEN, EDWARDSVILLE, AND DESTROYED A
DOCUMENT AND A PHOTOGRAPH WHICH WERE GOVERNMENT PROPERTY; ALSO
DISRUPTED ACTIVITIES OF THE BOARD AND CHANTED OBSCENE SLOGANS.
   SUBJECT IDENTIFIED FROM PHOTOGRAPHS AS LEADER OF
THIS GROUP AND PERSON WHO COMMITTED DESTRUCTIVE ACTS.
   AUSA J. WILLIAM ROBERTS, SDI, SPRINGFIELD, AUTHORIZED
PROSECUTION OF SUBJECT FOR VIOLATION TITLE EIGHTEEN, USC,
SECTION ONE THREE SIX ONE, AND TITLE FIFTY APPENDIX, USC,
SECTION FOUR SIX TWO, AND RECOMMENDED BOND FIFTEEN HUNDRED
DOLLARS CASH.
   COMPLAINT AND WARRANT BEING PREPARED TODAY AND
SUBJECT'S ARREST CONTEMPLATED. P.
END

DRL FBI WASH DC
                             SUPVR.

FEDERAL BUREAU OF INVESTIGATION

REPORTING OFFICE	OFFICE OF ORIGIN	DATE	INVESTIGATIVE PERIOD
SPRINGFIELD	SPRINGFIELD	5/13/70	5/7/70

TITLE OF CASE	REPORT MADE BY		TYPED BY
ROBERT ALLAN LAUD HUMPHREYS, aka Laud Humphreys	SA ███████	b7C	vh

CHARACTER OF CASE ███████

(DGP; SSA)

REFERENCE:

Springfield teletype to Bureau dated 5/7/70.

F0217

—P—

LEADS: SPRINGFIELD DIVISION

AT ALTON, ILLINOIS

Will conduct logical follow-up investigation to develop all
witnesses in this matter.

Will follow and report prosecutive action in this matter.

ACCOMPLISHMENTS CLAIMED					☒ NONE	ACQUIT-TALS	CASE HAS BEEN:		
CONVIC.	AUTO.	FUG.	FINES	SAVINGS	RECOVERIES				
							PENDING OVER ONE YEAR ☐YES ☒NO		
							PENDING PROSECUTION OVER SIX MONTHS ☐YES ☒NO		

APPROVED   SPECIAL AGENT IN CHARGE

DO NOT WRITE IN SPACES BELOW

COPIES MADE:
(2) - Bureau
1 - USA, Springfield
2 - Springfield (52-2805)

25- 612527 MCT-52
REC-101

10 MAY 21 1970

Dissemination Record of Attached Report			Notations
Agency		Icc by O-6 to Dept.	
Request Recd.		Atten: ██ ████	
Date Fwd.		Date sent 5/25/70	
How Fwd. JUN 5 1970		By C JD/s/f	
By			

—A*—
COVER PAGE

GPO : 1968 O - 298-865

2

TED STATES DEPARTMENT OF STICE
FEDERAL BUREAU OF INVESTIGATION

Copy to: 1 - USA, Springfield

Report of: SA ████████████ b7C
Date: May 13, 1970

Office: SPRINGFIELD

Field Office File #: SI 52-2805

Bureau File #:

Title: ROBERT ALLAN LAUD HUMPHREYS

Character: DESTRUCTION OF GOVERNMENT PROPERTY; SELECTIVE SERVICE ACT

Synopsis:

On 5/5/70 subject led a group of approximately 100 persons in a demonstration which resulted in the invasion of the private space of Local Boards 165-167, Edwardsville, Illinois, resulting in destruction of a document and a photograph which were government property. Subject also led group in disrupting activities of the Boards and chanting obscene slogans. Clerical personnel of Local Boards 165-167 identified subject from group photograph as leader of the group and person who committed destructive acts. AUSA J. WILLIAM ROBERTS, SDI, Springfield, authorized prosecution of subject for violation of Title 18, USC, Section 1361 and Title 50, Appendix, USC, Section 462. Bond recommended $1500. Authorized complaint filed before USC RONALD C. MATTAZ, Alton, Illinois 5/7/70 and warrant issued. Subject arrested same date by Buagents; appeared before USC MATTAZ and posted $1500 bond.

-p-

DETAILS:

3

SI 52-2805

PREDICATION:

Investigation in this matter is predicated upon information furnished by ████████████████ Local Boards 165-167, Edwardsville, Illinois, indicating that subject led a large group of persons into said Boards on 5/5/70; disrupted activities of the Boards and destroyed government property.

SI 52-2805

INVESTIGATION AT LOCAL BOARDS 165-167, EDWARDSVILLE, ILLINOIS

5

FEDERAL BUREAU OF INVESTIGATION

Date May 13, 1970

1

Selective Service System, advised that during the afternoon of May 5, 1970, LAUD HUMPHREYS led a group of approximately 100 persons into the private area of that board, at which time he led the group in chanting obscene slogans and intimidating employees of the board. ████████ stated that she recognized HUMPHREYS from photographs she has seen of him, and also viewed a group photograph containing several individuals and selected HUMPHREYS from the group.

████████ said that shortly after the group led by HUMPHREYS invaded Local Board 165-167, HUMPHREYS jumped up on a desk in the draft board, read a memorandum which was government property, and which consisted of a special memorandum to all local boards dated April 29, 1970 which is as follows:

"ILLINOIS HEADQUARTERS"
"SELECTIVE SERVICE SYSTEM"

"29 April 1970"

"SPECIAL MEMORANDUM TO ALL LOCAL BOARDS"

"SUBJECT: Induction Call for May 1970"

"1. Emergency action is necessary to insure that the May Induction Call for Illinois is met in full."

"2. Each local board should issue an Order to Report for Induction to all available registrants (Examined and Qualified) who are classified 1-A and 1-A-O with Random Sequence Numbers 1 through 145, to go with their regularly scheduled calls."

"3. If an increase in your call is necessary, order the registrant for induction and advise this Headquarters. Registrants must be given ten days notice."

"JOHN H. HAMMACK"
"State Director"

On 5/6/70 at Edwardsville, Illinois   File # 52-2805

by SA ████████   Date dictated 5/12/70

This document contains neither recommendations nor conclusions of the FBI. It is the property of the FBI and is loaned to your agency: it and its contents are not to be distributed outside your agency.

6

SI 52-2805
2

"Distribution: A."
"PM-5070"

b7C

                           said that after HUMPHREYS read the memorandum, he tore it in quarters and threw it on the floor.

         According to   HUMPHREYS thereafter ripped a photograph of President RICHARD M. NIXON from the wall of the draft board, smashed it on a desk, breaking the glass and thereafter tore the picture from the frame and tore the picture into several pieces.

                     concluded by stating that the group entered through a door marked no admittance, which door was waist high, but which was locked with a slide bolt from the inside.

FEDERAL BUREAU OF INVESTIGATION

Date___ May 13, 1970

1

_____ Local Boards 165-167
Selective Service System, viewed a group photograph depicting
a group of approximately 13 persons and selected from that
photograph the likeness of ROBERT ALLAN LAUD HUMPHREYS as
the person who led a group of approximately 100 individuals
in invading the private segment of Local Boards 165-167 on
May 5, 1970 and thereafter led the group in chanting obscene
slogans; and in general disrupting activities of the board.

_____ stated further that HUMPHREYS was the
individual who read an office memorandum of the board after
which he tore it into quarters and that he is the person who
destroyed a picture of President RICHARD M. NIXON which was
hanging on the wall of the draft board at the time of the
incident.

On___ 5/6/70 ___ at___ Edwardsville, Illinois ___ File #___ 52-2805

SA_____

by_____ Date dictated___ 5/12/70

8

FEDERAL BUREAU OF INVESTIGATION

Date _____ May 13, 1970

_b7C_

Selective Service System, viewed a group photograph depicting a group of approximately 13 persons and selected from that photograph the likeness of ROBERT ALLAN LAUD HUMPHREYS as the person who led a group of approximately 100 individuals in invading the private segment of Local Boards 165-167 on May 5, 1970 and thereafter led the group in chanting obscene slogans; and in general disrupting activities of the board.

_____ stated further that HUMPHREYS was the individual who read an office memorandum of the board after which he tore it into quarters and that he is the person who destroyed a picture of President RICHARD M. NIXON which was hanging on the wall of the draft board at the time of the incident.

On ___5/6/70___ at ___Edwardsville, Illinois___ File # ___52-2805___

by ___SA _____ _b7C_ Date dictated ___5/12/70___

This document contains neither recommendations nor conclusions of the FBI. It is the property of the FBI and is loaned to your agency; it and its contents are not to be distributed outside your agency.

FEDERAL BUREAU OF INVESTIGATION

1   Date   May 13, 1970   b7C

Selective Service System, viewed a group photograph depicting
a group of approximately 13 persons and selected from that
photograph the likeness of ROBERT ALLAN LAUD HUMPHREYS, as
the person who led a group of approximately 100 individuals
in invading the private segment of Local Boards 165-167 on
May 5, 1970 and thereafter led the group in chanting obscene
slogans; and in general disrupting activities of the board.

further stated that HUMPHREYS was the
individual who read an office memorandum of the board after
which he tore it into quarters and that he is the person who
destroyed a picture of President RICHARD M. NIXON which was
hanging on the wall of the draft board at the time of the
incident.

On 5/6/70 at Edwardsville, Illinois   File #   52-2805

by   SA   b7C

Date dictated   5/12/70

This document contains neither recommendations nor conclusions of the FBI. It is the property of the FBI and is loaned to your agency;
it and its contents are not to be distributed outside your agency.

10   8

FEDERAL BUREAU OF INVESTIGATION

Date May 13, 1970

1 ▮▮▮▮▮▮▮▮▮▮▮▮▮▮▮▮ Local Boards 165-167,
Selective Service System, viewed a group photograph depicting
a group of approximately 13 persons and selected from that
photograph the likeness of ROBERT ALLAN LAUD HUMPHREYS as
the person who led a group of approximately 100 individuals
in invading the private segment of Local Boards 165-167 on
May 5, 1970 and thereafter led the group in chanting obsdene
slogans; and in general disrupting activities of the board.

▮▮▮▮▮▮▮ further stated that HUMPHREYS was the
individual who read an office memorandum of the board after
which he tore it into quarters and that he is the person who
destroyed a picture of President RICHARD M. NIXON which was
hanging on the wall of the draft board at the time of the
incident.

On 5/6/70 at Edwardsville, Illinois File # 52-2805

by SA ▮▮▮▮▮▮▮▮▮▮▮▮ Date dictated 5/12/70

This document contains neither recommendations nor conclusions of the FBI. It is the property of the FBI and is loaned to your agency;
it and its contents are not to be distributed outside your agency.

SI 522805

PROSECUTIVE OPINION

On May 6, 1970 facts developed above were discussed with Assistant United States Attorney J. WILLIAM ROBERTS, Southern District of Illinois, Springfield. Mr. ROBERTS advised that he would authorize prosecution of the subject for a violation of Title 18, USC, Section 1361 and for a violation of Title 50 Appendix, USC, Section 462. Mr. ROBERTS recommended a bond of $1500 cash.

On May 7, 1970 an authorized complaint was filed before USC RONALD C. MATTAZ, Alton, Illinois charging subject with a violation of Title 18, USC, Section 1361 and violation of Title 50, Appendix, USC, Section 462, and a warrant was issued.

On the same date, ROBERT ALLAN LAUD HUMPHREYS was arrested by SAS ███████████████████████ and ██████████████ at his residence, 14 Biscayne Drive, Edwards-ville, Illinois.

b7C

12

FEDERAL BUREAU OF INVESTIGATION

1   Date: May 13, 1970

ROBERT ALLAN LAUD HUMPHREYS, subsequent to his arrest at Edwardsville, Illinois, was transported by Bucar to Alton, Illinois, at which time he was taken to the Alton Police Department for the purpose of obtaining photographs and fingerprints of HUMPHREYS.

During the trip from Edwardsville to Alton, Illinois, no discussion was had with HUMPHREYS which would be germane to this particular matter.

Prior to taking photographs and fingerprints, and Advice of Rights form was furnished to HUMPHREYS. He read the form, acknowledged its contents, and stated he would refuse to waive his rights.

The following description of HUMPHREYS was obtained at the time of photographing and fingerprinting at the Alton, Illinois Police Department.

Race:	White
Sex:	Male
Ht:	5'9½"
Wt:	165 lbs.
Hair:	Brown
Eyes:	Brown
Age:	39
DOB:	10/16/30
POB:	Chickasha, Oklahoma
Marital status:	Married
Occupation:	Sociology Professor
Residence:	14 Biscayne, Edwardsville, Ill.

On 5/7/70 at Alton, Illinois

File # 52-2805

by SAS ▮▮▮▮▮▮▮▮▮▮ and ▮▮▮▮▮▮▮ b7C te dictated 5/12/70

11

SI:52-2805

On May 7, 1970, subject was taken before United States Commissione
ROBALD C. MATTAZ at Alton, Illinois, at which time he refused to
waive preliminary hearing and posted bond in the amount of
$1500.

19

OPTIONAL FORM NO. 10
MAY 1962 EDITION
GSA FPMR (41 CFR) 101-11.6

UNITED STATES ⟨ ⟩RNMENT

Memorandum

TO : DIRECTOR, FBI (25-612529)   DATE: 5/26/70

FROM : SAC, SPRINGFIELD (52-2805) - P -

SUBJECT: ROBERT ALLAN LAUD HUMPHREYS, aka
DGP; SSA

     Facts developed during investigation presented to
Federal Grand Jury, SDI, Springfield, Illinois, 5/26/70, and
Federal Grand Jury returned True Bill indicting subject for
violation Title 18, USC, Section 1361, and Title 50 Appendix,
USC, Section 462.

     Above submitted to the Bureau for information in view
of subject's status as a sociology professor at Southern Illinois
University, Edwardsville, Illinois.

②- Bureau (25-612529)
3 - Springfield (2: 52-2805)
          (1: 105-3118)   REC- 91
RCH/smr
(5)

    0-1 to __S.I.__
    RE: _____
    Date sent _6/8/70_
    By _WRH/s/c_

9 MAY 28 1970

1 JUN 10 1970

FD-263 (Rev. 3-8-67)

FEDERAL BUREAU OF INVESTIGATION

REPORTING OFFICE	OFFICE OF ORIGIN	DATE	INVESTIGATIVE PERIOD
SPRINGFIELD	SPRINGFIELD	6/30/70	5/26 – 6/11/70

TITLE OF CASE	REPORT MADE BY		TYPED BY
ROBERT ALLAN LAUD HUMPHREYS, Aka	SA ███████ b7c		bji

CHARACTER OF CASE

DGP; SSA

REFERENCE:

       b7c

    Springfield report of SA ███████ dated 5/13/70;

-P-

LEADS: SPRINGFIELD DIVISION

AT ALTON, ILLINOIS

      Will follow and report prosecutive action in this
matter.

		ACCOMPLISHMENTS CLAIMED		NONE		ACQUIT-TALS	CASE HAS BEEN:	
CONVIC.	AUTO.	FUG.	FINES	SAVINGS	RECOVERIES		PENDING OVER ONE YEAR ☐YES ☒NO	
							PENDING PROSECUTION	
							OVER SIX MONTHS ☐YES ☒NO	

APPROVED   SPECIAL AGENT IN CHARGE   DO NOT WRITE IN SPACES BELOW

COPIES MADE:

    ② – Bureau (25-612529)
    1 – USA, Springfield
    2 – Springfield (52-2805)

   25-612529   REC-23

  EX-117

B JUL 2 1970

Dissemination Record of Attached Report				Notations	
Agency					
Request Recd.					
Date Fwd.					
How Fwd.					

B 51 JUL 13 1970

-A*-
COVER PAGE

☆ U.S. GOVERNMENT PRINTING OFFICE : 1967 O—275-977

UNITED STATES DEPARTMENT OF JUSTICE
FEDERAL BUREAU OF INVESTIGATION

Copy to: 1 - USA, Springfield

Report of: SA ██████████████ *b7C*   Office: SPRINGFIELD
Date: June 30, 1970

Field Office File #:   SI 52-2805   Bureau File #: 25-612529

Title: ROBERT ALLAN LAUD HUMPHREYS

Character: DESTRUCTION OF GOVERNMENT PROPERTY; SELECTIVE
SERVICE ACT

Synopsis: True bill of indictment returned by Federal Grand Jury,
Southern District of Illinois, Springfield, Illinois, on
5/26/70 charging subject with violation Title 18, USC,
Section 1361 and Title 50, Appendix, USC, Section 462.
Subject arraigned before Judge OMER POOS, Southern District
of Illinois, at Alton, Illinois, on 6/11/70 accompanied by
his attorney at which time he entered a plea of not guilty
to the charges.

-P-

DETAILS:

On May 26, 1970, the facts developed during this
investigation were presented to a Federal Grand Jury sitting
at Springfield, Illinois, in the Southern District of Illinois.
The Federal Grand Jury on the same date returned a true bill of
indictment charging subject with a violation of Title 18, United
States Code, Section 1361, and Title 50, Appendix, United States
Code, Section 462.

On June 11, 1970, subject appeared in U. S. District
Court, Southern District of Illinois, at Alton, Illinois, before
Judge OMER-POOS accompanied by his attorney RICHARD SHAIKEWITZ
at which time he entered a plea of not guilty to the specified
charges.

-1*-

17

U. S. GOVERNMENT PRINTING OFFICE : 1969 O - 351-076

FD-263 (Rev. 3-8-67)

FEDERAL BUREAU OF INVESTIGATION

REPORTING OFFICE	OFFICE OF ORIGIN	DATE	INVESTIGATIVE PERIOD
SPRINGFIELD	SPRINGFIELD	8/20/70	8/19/70

TITLE OF CASE	REPORT MADE BY	TYPED BY
ROBERT ALLAN LAUD HUMPHREYS, Aka	SA ██████████ b7c	bji

CHARACTER OF CASE

DGP; SSA

REFERENCE:

Springfield report of SA ██████████ b7c dated 6/30/70.

–P–

LEAD: SPRINGFIELD DIVISION

AT ALTON, ILLINOIS

Will follow and report prosecutive action in this matter.

ACCOMPLISHMENTS CLAIMED						ACQUIT-TALS	CASE HAS BEEN:		
CONVIC.	AUTO.	FUG.	FINES	SAVINGS	RECOVERIES		PENDING OVER ONE YEAR ☐YES ☐NO		
							PENDING PROSECUTION OVER SIX MONTHS ☐YES ☐NO		

APPROVED _____ SPECIAL AGENT IN CHARGE

DO NOT WRITE IN SPACES BELOW

COPIES MADE:

2 - Bureau (25-612529)
1 - USA, Springfield
2 - Springfield (52-2805)

25-612529-5 REC. 17

EX 106

18 AUG 24 1970

SIX

Dissemination Record of Attached Report

Agency					Notations
Request Recd.					
Date Fwd.					
How Fwd.					

6 - SEP 3 1970

–A*–
COVER PAGE

* U.S. GOVERNMENT PRINTING OFFICE : 1967 O—273-877

U. I ED STATES DEPARTMENT OF JSTICE
FEDERAL BUREAU OF INVESTIGATION

Copy to:	1 – USA, Springfield		
		b7C	
Report of:	SA ▮▮▮▮▮▮▮▮▮▮	Office:	SPRINGFIELD
Date:	August 20, 1970		
Field Office File #:	SI 52-2805	Bureau File #: 25-612529	
Title:	ROBERT ALLAN LAUD HUMPHREYS		

Character: DESTRUCTION OF GOVERNMENT PROPERTY; SELECTIVE
SERVICE ACT

Synopsis: Records of USA's Office, SDI, Springfield, Illinois, disclose
no trial date set in this matter. However, subject will
appear in USDC, SDI, Springfield, on 8/26/70, at which time a
hearing will be held on motions entered by defendant.

-P-

DETAILS:

       On August 19, 1970, ▮▮▮▮▮▮▮▮▮▮▮▮▮▮▮▮▮▮▮▮
to the United States Attorney, Southern District of Illinois,
Springfield, Illinois, advised that no trial date has been set
in this matter. She advised, however, that a hearing has been
scheduled to be held on August 26, 1970, at which time the
subject will appear with his attorney for a hearing on motions
filed by him.

-1*-

FD-263 (Rev. 3-8-67)

FEDERAL BUREAU OF INVESTIGATION

REPORTING OFFICE	OFFICE OF ORIGIN	DATE	INVESTIGATIVE PERIOD
SPRINGFIELD	SPRINGFIELD	10/27/70	9/1/70 - 10/20/70

TITLE OF CASE	REPORT		TYPED BY
ROBERT ALLAN LAUD HUMPHREYS, aka	SA ▮▮▮▮▮▮ *b7c*		mpb

CHARACTER OF CASE

TGP; SSA

REFERENCES:

Springfield report of SA ▮▮▮▮▮▮▮ *b7c* 8/20/70.

- P -

LEADS:

SPRINGFIELD DIVISION

At Alton, Illinois

Will follow and report prosecutive action in this matter.

ACCOMPLISHMENTS CLAIMED NONE.					ACQUIT-TALS	CASE HAS BEEN:	
CONVIC.	AUTO.	FUG.	FINES	SAVINGS	RECOVERIES		PENDING OVER ONE YEAR ☐YES ☒NO
							PENDING PROSECUTION OVER SIX MONTHS ☐YES ☒NO

APPROVED _____ SPECIAL AGENT IN CHARGE

DO NOT WRITE IN SPACES BELOW

COPIES MADE:

(2) - Bureau (25-612529)

1 - USA, Springfield

2 - Springfield (52-2805)

25-612529 - 6 REC- 79

22 OCT 29 1970 EX-106

Dissemination Record of Attached Report	Notations
Agency	O-6D to Szukelwicz
Request Recd.	11/19/70
Date Fwd.	OSD/bla
How Fwd.	
By	- A* -

66 NOV 01 1970

20

- COVER PAGE -

※ U.S. GOVERNMENT PRINTING OFFICE : 1967 O—273-877

UNITED STATES DEPARTMENT OF JUSTICE
FEDERAL BUREAU OF INVESTIGATION

Copy to: 1 - USA, Springfield

Report of: SA _____ *b7C*   Office: SPRINGFIELD
Date: October 27, 1970

Field Office File #: SI 52-2805   Bureau File #:25-612529

Title: ROBERT ALLAN LAUD HUMPHREYS

Character: THEFT OF GOVERNMENT PROPERTY;
SELECTIVE SERVICE ACT

Synopsis:
Hearing on motions of defendant heard August 27, 1970. Trial
date set for December 2, 1970.

- P -

DETAILS: *b7C*

            On September 1, 1970, _____
to the United States Attorney, Southern District of Illinois,
Springfield, Illinois, advised that a hearing was held on defense
motions in the matter of ROBERT ALLAN LAUD HUMPHREYS on August 27,
1970, before Judge OMER POOS with the following results:

Motions Allowed

            1. Trial by jury

            2. Government to furnish defendant with copy of all
admissions and confessions made by defendant, concerning offenses
charged which are in the possession of the Government.

            3. Suppression of confessions and admissions continued.

            4. Ruling reserved on suppression of real and tangible
evidence.

21

U. S. GOVERNMENT PRINTING OFFICE : 1969 O - 351-078

FI 52-2805

5. Defendant allowed to inspect and copy documents and photographs, inspect all real and tangible evidence and premises of occurrance allowed to see results of any scientific tests.

6. Government required to produce transcripts of any electronic eavesdropping of conversations in which defendant participated, or which occurred on his premises.

7. Clerk of Court ordered to furnish information and defense counsel relating to manner of selection of jury array.

8. Government ordered to produce any information in its files which is material to the case and tends to exculpate the defendant.

9. Government ordered to produce Jencks Act statements at trial.

10. Bill of Particulars - Government ordered to:
     A. Show defendant premises
     B. Show defendant memo
     C. Show defendant photograph, frame, etc.
     D. State time of occurrence charged
     E. State in general from the acts which are alleged to constitute violations of the law.

11. Clerk, United States Attorney's Office and Federal Bureau of Investigation ordered not to hold press conference on evidentiary matters relating to trial. Court specifically allowed divulgence of any matter of public record.

12. Motions which are allowed are to be considered continuing.

13. All other motions denied.

On October 20, 1970, Assistant United States Attorney J. WILLIAM ROBERTS, Southern District of Illinois, Springfield, Illinois, advised that trial is set in this matter to begin at Springfield, Illinois, on December 2, 1970.

- 2* -

22

GSA FPMR (41 CFR) 101-11.5

UNITED STATES GOVERNMENT

Memorandum

TO : DIRECTOR, FBI (25-612529)   DATE: 12/3/70

FROM : SAC, SPRINGFIELD (52-2805) -P-

SUBJECT: ROBERT ALLAN LAUD HUMPHREYS, aka
DGP; SSA

        Re Springfield report of SA ▮▮▮▮▮▮▮▮ b7C
dated 10/27/70.

        Trial commenced in this matter on 12/2/70. Upon
reconvening USDC, SDI, Springfield, morning 12/3/70, subject
entered motion to change plea regarding Count 1 of indictment
from not guilty to guilty. Judge OMER POOS accepted plea
of guilty and ordered pre-sentence investigation. USA's
Office, Springfield, advised that upon sentencing Count 2
of the indictment will be nolle prossed.

        Upon sentencing a closing report will be submitted.

REC-1 25-612529-7

4 DEC 7 1970

ST-111

2 - Bureau (25-612529)
2 - Springfield (52-2805)
RCH/ssj
(4)

5 6 DEC 15 1970

23   *Buy U.S. Savings Bonds Regularly on the Payroll Savings Plan*

FEDERAL BUREAU OF INVESTIGATION

REPORTING OFFICE	OFFICE OF ORIGIN	DATE	INVESTIGATIVE PERIOD
SPRINGFIELD	SPRINGFIELD	1/15/71	12/3/70 - 1/7/71

TITLE OF CASE	REPORT MADE BY	TYPED BY
ROBERT ALLAN LAUD HUMPHREYS, aka,	SA ██████████ b7C	ral
	CHARACTER OF CASE	
	DGP; SSA	

b7C

REFERENCES: Springfield report of SA ██████████ 0/27/70.
Springfield letter to the Bureau, 12/3/70.

- C -

ENCLOSURES:

Enclosed for the Bureau is one copy of Disposition Sheet
reflecting sentence received by subject.

ACCOMPLISHMENTS CLAIMED	☐ NONE		ACQUIT-TALS	CASE HAS BEEN:
CONVIC.	AUTO.	FUG.	FINES	SAVINGS	RECOVERIES			PENDING OVER ONE YEAR ☐YES ☐NO
								PENDING PROSECUTION OVER SIX MONTHS ☐YES ☐NO

APPROVED	SPECIAL AGENT IN CHARGE	DO NOT WRITE IN SPACES BELOW

COPIES MADE:

2 - Bureau (25-612529) (Enc. 1)

1 - USA, Springfield

1 - Springfield (52-2805)

25-612529-8

REC
EX-115
9 JAN 18 1971

Dissemination Record of Attached Report					Notations
Agency					
Request Recd.					
Date Fwd.					
How Fwd.					
By					

24 62FEB1 1971

- A* -
COVER PAGE

GPO : 1968 O - 299-883

UNITED STATES DEPARTMENT OF JUSTICE
FEDERAL BUREAU OF INVESTIGATION

Copy to: 1 - USA, SPRINGFIELD

Report of: SA ████████████ b7C   Office: SPRINGFIELD
Date: JANUARY 15, 1971

Field Office File #:   SI 52-2805   Bureau File #:   25-612529

Title: ROBERT ALLAN LAUD HUMPHREYS

Character: DESTRUCTION OF GOVERNMENT PROPERTY;
             SELECTIVE SERVICE ACT

Synopsis: Subject appeared in USDC, SDI, Springfield, 12/3/70,
             entered motion to change plea regarding count one
             from not guilty to guilty. Subject appeared in USDC,
             SDI, Springfield, on 1/7/71, at which time sentenced
             to one year custody of Attorney General; first four
             months of which to be spent in jail type institution,
             the balance suspended and placed on three years probation.
             Sentence imposed for violation Title 18, USC, Section
             1361. Count two of indictment concerning violation of
             Title 50, Appendix, USC, Section 462, nolle prossed by
             United States Attorney's Office.

                          - C -

DETAILS:

        Trial was commenced in this matter on December 2,
1970, and on December 3, 1970, the subject, with his
attorney, entered a motion before United States District
Judge OMER POOS, in United States District Court, Southern
District of Illinois, Springfield, Illinois, to change
his plea on Count One of the indictment from not guilty
to guilty. This involved a violation of Title 18, United
States Code, Section 1361. The plea was accepted by
Judge POOS on December 3, 1970.

25

SI 52-2805

On January 7, 1971, the subject, with his attorney, appeared in United States District Court, Southern District of Illinois, Springfield, Illinois, before Judge POOS and after hearings in mitigation and aggravation, subject was sentenced to a term of one year in the custody of the Attorney General; the first four months of which were to be spent in a jail type institution, with the balance suspended and the subject placed on three years probation.

Count Two of the indictment which involved a violation of Title 50, Appendix, United States Code, Section 462, was nolle prossed by Assistant United States Attorney J. WILLIAM ROBERTS after sentencing of the subject.

- 2* -

26

OPTIONAL FORM NO. 10
MAY 1962 EDITION
GSA FPMR (41 CFR) 101-11.6

UNITED STATES GOVERNMENT

Memorandum

TO : DIRECTOR, FBI

DATE: June 8, 1970

FROM : SAC, SPRINGFIELD (105-3118) (P)

SUBJECT: ROBERT ALLAN LAUD HUMPHREYS, aka
Laud Humphreys
SM - MISCELLANEOUS

Re Springfield letter and LHM dated January 19,
1970, captioned, "COMMITTEE FOR INTERNATIONAL CONCERN,
SOUTHERN ILLINOIS UNIVERSITY, EDWARDSVILLE, ILLINOIS (SIUE)."

Enclosed herewith for the Bureau are the original
and 10 copies of an LHM captioned as above, together with
two copies of an FD-376 and two copies of an FD-397,
recommending subject for inclusion in the Agitator Index
of the Springfield Division.

The LHM has been disseminated locally to United
States Attorney, Springfield; OSI, Chanute Air Force Base,
Rantoul; NISO, Chicago; Secret Service, Springfield; and
MI Groups, Evanston, Illinois and St. Louis, Missouri.

The enclosed LHM summarizes known activities of
the subject in view of his recent activities and in order
to support the recommendation for his inclusion in the
Agitator Index.
b2
Source mentioned in LHM is as follows: b7D

LEAD

SPRINGFIELD DIVISION

At Alton, Illinois

Will await Bureau approval for subject's inclusion
in the Agitator Index.

ENCLOSURE

ALL INFORMATION CONTAINED
HEREIN IS UNCLASSIFIED
DATE 1-19-79 BY Sp-5 R.M/mz

MCT-3   100 - 459062

REC-38

2 - Bureau (Encl. 15) (RM)
3 - Springfield (105-3118)   Copy to RAI SS
1 - (66-1967)   by routing slip for
RCH/es   info action
(5)   date 6/9/70
                               by

16 JUN 11 1970

INT SEC,

5 JUN 24 1970

27

FD-376 (Rev. 4-25-68)

UNITED STATES DEPARTMENT OF JUSTICE

FEDERAL BUREAU OF INVESTIGATION

In Reply, Please Refer to   WASHINGTON, D.C. 20535
File No.
Director   **June 8, 1970**
United States Secret Service
Department of the Treasury
Washington, D. C. 20220

Dear Sir:

        The information furnished herewith concerns an individual who is believed to be
covered by the agreement between the FBI and Secret Service concerning Presidential protection, and to fall within the category or categories checked.

1. ☐ Has attempted or threatened bodily harm to any government official or employee,
   including foreign government officials residing in or planning an imminent visit to the
   U. S., because of his official status.

2. ☐ Has attempted or threatened to redress a grievance against any public official by other
   than legal means.

3. ☐ Because of background is potentially dangerous; or has been identified as member or
   participant in communist movement; or has been under active investigation as member
   of other group or organization inimical to U. S.

4. ☐ U. S. citizens or residents who defect from the U. S. to countries in the Soviet or
   Chinese Communist blocs and return.

5. ☒ Subversives, ultrarightists, racists and fascists who meet one or more of the following
   criteria:

   (a) ☐ Evidence of emotional instability (including unstable residence and
        employment record) or irrational or suicidal behavior:
   (b) ☒ Expressions of strong or violent anti-U. S. sentiment;
   (c) ☒ Prior acts (including arrests or convictions) or conduct or statements
        indicating a propensity for violence and antipathy toward good order
        and government.

6. ☐ Individuals involved in illegal bombing or illegal bomb-making.

Photograph ☐ has been furnished ☐ enclosed ☐ is not available
☐ may be available through _____

_____ .

                          Very truly yours,

                              John Edgar Hoover
                                  Director

1 - Special Agent in Charge (Enclosure(s)
    U. S. Secret Service

Enclosure(s)
                    *(Upon removal of classified enclosures, if any, this transmittal form
28   becomes UNCLASSIFIED.)*

UNITED STATES DEPARTMENT OF JUSTICE

FEDERAL BUREAU OF INVESTIGATION

Springfield, Illinois
June 8, 1970

In Reply, Please Refer to
File No.

ROBERT ALLAN LAUD HUMPHREYS,
ALSO KNOWN AS
LAUD HUMPHREYS

b2
b7D

▓▓▓▓▓▓▓▓▓▓▓▓▓▓▓▓▓▓▓▓▓▓▓▓ who has
furnished reliable information in the past, advised in
January, 1970, that Laud Humphreys, a Professor of History
and Sociology at Southern Illinois University, Edwardsville,
Illinois (SIU-E), is a sponsor of the Committee for
International Concern on the campus of SIU-E and has been
active in promoting activities of Vietnam Moratorium
Committee within the Committee for International Concern.

A characterization of the Committee for
International Concern appears in the appendix.

On ▓▓▓▓▓▓▓▓▓▓▓▓ advised that Humphreys continued
to be a faculty sponsor for the Committee for International
Concern and was its nominal leader. He said that Humphreys
has definitely moved the philosophy and motives of the group
to the left of center and has been obscene and vituperative
in remarks concerning the present administration and United
States policies.

b2
b7D

On May 7, 1970, ▓▓▓▓▓▓▓▓▓▓▓▓▓▓▓▓▓▓ Local
Draft Board No. 165-167, Edwardsville, Illinois, advised
that on the afternoon of May 5, 1970, Humphreys led a group
of approximately 100 persons into the Draft Board; that the
group forced its way into the private area of the Board
and thereafter responding to leadership of Humphreys,
harassed the clerical employees of the Draft Board for a
period of approximately 15-20 minutes, which harassment
included the chanting of obscene slogans and threatening
gestures and remarks concerning possible destruction of
Selective Service records.

b7C
b7D

ALL INFORMATION CONTAINED
HEREIN IS UNCLASSIFIED
DATE 11-14-79 BY SP-5 RJL/MN

100 - 459062 - 7/

ENCLOSURE

29

ROBERT ALLAN LAUD HUMPHREYS,
ALSO KNOWN AS
LAUD HUMPHREYS
_____

████████████ further stated that Humphreys picked   67C
up a memorandum which was the property of the United States   67D
government, read it to the group in a loud voice and thereafter tore it in quarters. She said that he then tore a
photograph of President Nixon from the wall of the Draft
Board; smashed the glass in the picture; tore the picture
from its mounting and then tore the picture into shreads.

On May 7, 1970, Assistant United States Attorney
J. William Roberts, Southern District of Illinois, Springfield,
Illinois, authorized prosecution of Humphreys for a violation
of Title 18, United States Code, Section 1361, and Title 50,
Appendix, United States Code, Section 462. On the same
date an authorized complaint was filed before United States
Commissioner Ronald C. Mottaz at Alton, Illinois, and a
warrant was issued.

On the same date, Humphreys was arrested by
Special Agents of the Federal Bureau of Investigation
pursuant to the above described complaint and warrant.
He was taken before Commissioner Mottaz and posted $1,500.00
bond.

On May 26, 1970, a Federal Grand Jury sitting at
Springfield, Illinois, in the Southern District of Illinois,
heard facts concerning the invasion of the Draft Board at
Edwardsville, Illinois, and returned a True Bill of
indictment charging Humphreys with a violation of Title 18,
United States Code, Section 1361, and Title 50, Appendix,
United States Code, Section 462.

The following description of Humphreys was
obtained through observation and interrogation:

Race	White
Sex	Male
Nationality	American
Height	5' 9½"
Weight	165 pounds
Hair	Brown
Eyes	Brown
Age	39
Date of Birth	October 16, 1930
Place of Birth	Chickasha, Oklahoma

30

2

ROBERT ALLAN LAUD HUMPHREYS,
ALSO KNOWN AS
LAUD HUMPHREYS

Marital Status	Married
Occupation	Sociology Professor
Residence	14 Biscayne Drive
	Edwardsville, Illinois

3

31

ROBERT ALLAN LAUD HUMPHREYS,
ALSO KNOWN AS
LAUD HUMPHREYS

A P P E N D I X

COMMITTEE FOR INTERNATIONAL CONCERN
SOUTHERN ILLINOIS UNIVERSITY
EDWARDSVILLE, ILLINOIS

b7C
b7D

Southern Illinois University, Edwardsville, Illinois (SIU-E),
has advised that the Committee for International Concern
(CIC) was established on the campus of SIU-E during the
school year 1967-68 as an outgrowth of the foreign policy
club attached to the Social Sciences Division of the
University. He stated that CIC is a recognized student
organization and as such, has access to meeting halls and
the school newspaper, "The Alestle". ▮▮▮▮▮ advised that
until the late summer of 1969 the activities of CIC were
innocuous and certainly not controversial. He said, however,
since approximately August, 1969, the student and faculty
leaders of the organization have taken a definite stand with
regard to foreign policy and have moved the CIC to the left
of center politically so that the organization at this time
supports the Vietnam Moratorium Committee; has entertained
representatives from other left wing groups like the Students
for a Democratic Society (SDS) and the Young Socialist
Alliance (YSA).

Characterizations of the SDS and YSA are attached.

A P P E N D I X

32

ROBERT ALLAN LAUD HUMPHREYS,   A P P E N D I X
ALSO KNOWN AS
LAUD HUMPHREYS

STUDENTS FOR A DEMOCRATIC SOCIETY

A source has advised that the Students for a
Democratic Society (SDS), as presently regarded, came into
being at a founding convention held June, 1962, at Port
Huron, Michigan. From an initial posture of "participatory
democracy" the line of the national leadership has revealed
a growing Marxist-Leninist adherence which currently calls
for the building of a revolutionary youth movement.
Concurrently, the program of SDS has evolved from civil rights
struggles to an anti-Vietnam war stance to an advocacy of a
militant anti-imperialist position. China, Vietnam and
Cuba are regarded as the leaders of worldwide struggles
against United States imperialism whereas the Soviet Union
is held to be revisionist and also imperialist.

At the June, 1969, SDS National Convention,
Progressive Labor Party (PLP) forces in the organization
were expelled. As a result, the National Office (NO) group
maintained its National Headquarters at 1608 West Madison
Street, Chicago, and the PLP faction set up headquarters
in Cambridge, Massachusetts. This headquarters subsequently
moved to Boston. Each group elected its own national officers,
which include three national secretaries and a National
Interim Committee of eight. Both the NO forces and the PLP
forces claim to be the true SDS. Both groups also print
their versions of "New Left Notes" which sets forth the line
and the program of the particular faction. The NO version
of "New Left Notes" was recently printed under the title
"The Fire Next Time" to achieve a broader mass appeal.

Two major factions have developed internally within
the NO group, namely, the Weatherman or Revolutionary Youth
Movement (RYM) I faction, and the RYM II faction. Weatherman
is action-oriented upholding Castro's position that the duty
of revolutionaries is to make revolution. Weatherman is
regarded by RYM II as an adventuristic, elitist faction
which denies the historical role of the working class as the
base for revolution. RYM II maintains that revolution,
although desired, is not possible under present conditions,

A P P E N D I X

ROBERT ALLAN LAUD HUMPHREYS,   A P P E N D I X
ALSO KNOWN AS
LAUD HUMPHREYS

STUDENTS FOR A DEMOCRATIC SOCIETY

hence emphasizes organizing and raising the political
consciousness of the working class upon whom they feel
successful revolution depends. Although disclaiming control
and domination by the Communist Party, USA, leaders in these
two factions have in the past proclaimed themselves to be
communists and to follow the precepts of a Marxist-Leninist
philosophy, along pro-Chinese communist lines.

        A second source has advised that the PLP faction
which is more commonly known as the Worker Student Alliance
is dominated and controlled by members of the PLP, who are
required to identify themselves with the pro-Chinese Marxist-
Leninist philosophy of the PLP. They advocate that an
alliance between workers and students is vital to the bringing
about of a revolution in the United States.

        SDS regions and university and college chapters,
although operating under the outlines of the SDS National
Constitution, are autonomous in nature and free to carry
out independent policy reflective of local conditions.
Because of this autonomy internal struggles reflecting the
major factional interests of SDS have occurred at the chapter
level since the beginning of the 1969-70 school year.

        A characterization of PLP is attached.

                                        A P P E N D I X

34

ROBERT ALLAN LAUD HUMPHREYS,   **A P P E N D I X**
ALSO KNOWN AS
LAUD HUMPHREYS

PROGRESSIVE LABOR PARTY (PLP)

"The New York Times" city edition, Tuesday,
April 20, 1965, page 27, reported that a new party of
"revolutionary socialism" was formally founded on April 18,
1965, under the name of the PLP which had been known as the
Progressive Labor Movement.

According to the article, "The Progressive Labor
Movement was founded in 1962, by Milton Rosen and Mortimer
Scheer after they were expelled from the Communist Party
of the United States for assertedly following the Chinese
Communist line."

A source advised on June 3, 1968, that the PLP
held its Second National Convention in New York City,
May 31 to June 2, 1968, at which time the PLP reasserted
its objective of the establishment of a militant working
class movement based on Marxism-Leninism. This is to be
accomplished through the Party's over-all revolutionary
strategy of raising the consciousness of the people and
helping to provide ideological leadership in the working
class struggle for state power.

The source also advised that at the Second National
Convention Milton Rosen was unanimously re-elected National
Chairman of the PLP and Levi Laub, Fred Jerome, Jared Israel,
William Epton, Jacob Rosen, Jeffrey Gordon, and Walter Linder
were elected as the National Committee to lead the PLP until
the next convention.

The PLP publishes "Progressive Labor," a bimonthly
magazine; "World Revolution," a quarterly periodical; and
"Challenge-Desafio," a monthly newspaper.

The April, 1969, issue of "Challenge-Desafio" sets
forth that "Challenge is dedicated to the peoples fight for
a new-way of life--where the working men and women control
their own homes and factories; where they themselves make
up the entire government on every level and control the

A P P E N D I X

ROBERT ALLAN LAUD HUMPHREYS,
ALSO KNOWN AS
LAUD HUMPHREYS

A P P E N D I X

PROGRESSIVE LABOR PARTY (PLP)

schools, courts, police and all institutions which are now
used to control them."

      Source advised on May 8, 1969, that the PLP
utilizes an address of General Post Office Box 808, Brooklyn,
New York, and also utilizes an office in Room 617, 1 Union
Square West, New York, New York.

A P P E N D I X

ROBERT ALLAN LAUD HUMPHREYS,   **A P P E N D I X**
ALSO KNOWN AS
LAUD HUMPHREYS

YOUNG SOCIALIST ALLIANCE

A source advised on May 15, 1969, that the Young
Socialist Alliance (YSA) maintains its national headquarters
at 41 Union Square West, New York, New York, and has as its
official publication the "Young Socialist." The YSA is the
youth organization of the Socialist Workers Party (SWP) and
has been described by the SWP as the main recruiting ground
for the SWP.

The SWP has been designated pursuant to Executive
Order 10450.

This document contains neither recommendations nor
conclusions of the FBI. It is the property of the FBI and
is loaned to your agency; it and its contents. are not to
be distributed outside your agency.

A P P E N D I X

9*

FD-36 (Rev. 4-2-68)
OPTIONAL FORM NO. 10
MAY 1962 EDITION
GSA GEN. REG. NO. 27

UNITED STATES GOVERNMENT

Memorandum

TO : Director, FBI (Bufile-

DATE: June 8, 1970

FROM : SAC, SPRINGFIELD (105-3118) (P)

Card filed:
Card sent DB
6/25/70

OK for AI
5

SUBJECT: ROBERT ALLAN LAUD HUMPHREYS, aka
Laud Humphreys
SM - MISCELLANEOUS

AGITATOR INDEX

[X] New Subject   [ ] Change   [ ] Delete

Name	FBI Number
ROBERT ALLAN LAUD HUMPHREYS	

Aliases

LAUD HUMPHREYS

ALL INFORMATION CONTAINED
HEREIN IS UNCLASSIFIED
DATE 11-15-79 BY SP-5 RJE/14R

Citizenship
[X] Native Born   [ ] Naturalized   [ ] Alien

Subject also on	Race	Sex
[ ] SI [ ] RI	White	[X] Male [ ] Female

Organizational Affiliation

[ ] 01 ANP	[ ] 07 KLAN	[ ] 12 PLP	[ ] 17 SNCC
[ ] 02 AVN	[ ] 08 LA	[ ] 13 PRN	[ ] 18 SWP
[ ] 03 BNAT	[ ] 09 MIN	[ ] 14 RAM	[ ] 19 WWP
[ ] 04 BPP	[ ] 10 NOI	[ ] 15 SCLC	[X] 99 MISC
[ ] 05 COM	[ ] 11 NSRP	[ ] 16 SDS	(Specify)
[ ] 06 CORE			Committee for International Concern (CIC).

Date of Birth	Place of Birth	
10/16/30	Chickasha, Oklahoma	

Position in Organization	Occupation, Business Address (Show Name of Employing Concern)
Faculty sponsor	Sociology Professor Southern Illinois University Edwardsville, Illinois EX 106

Residence Address
14 Biscayne Drive
Edwardsville, Illinois

REG- 86 100-459062-2

391260

REGISTERED MAIL

(2) - Bureau (RM)
2 - Springfield (105-3118)
RCH/es

16 JUN 11 1970

54 JUN 30 1970

3B

SI 105-3118

SUCCINCT SUMMARY:

Subject has been a faculty sponsor for the Committee for International Concern, Southern Illinois University, Edwardsville, Illinois (SIU-E), and has through his leadership moved this organization to the far left politically. Further, the subject grafically illustrated a propensity to agitate by his leadership of a group into the Local Draft Board, Edwardsville, Illinois, where they disrupted activities of the Board and destroyed government property.

In view of subject's activities and propensity for agitation, it is recommended that he be included in the Agitator Index of the Springfield Division.

Addendum

Subject was indicted by FGJ re above act at Draft Board on 5/26/70 and currently out on $1500 bond.

2*

39

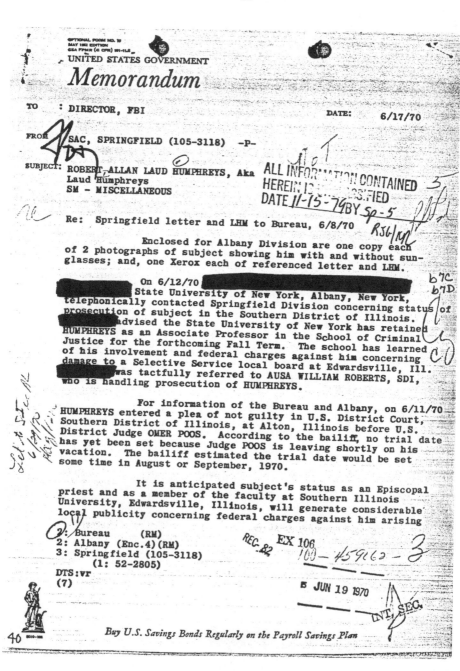

OPTIONAL FORM NO. 10
MAY 1962 EDITION
GSA FPMR (41 CFR) 101-11.6

UNITED STATES GOVERNMENT

Memorandum

TO : DIRECTOR, FBI

DATE: 6/17/70

FROM : SAC, SPRINGFIELD (105-3118) -P-

SUBJECT: ROBERT ALLAN LAUD HUMPHREYS, Aka
Laud Humphreys
SM - MISCELLANEOUS

ALL INFORMATION CONTAINED
HEREIN IS UNCLASSIFIED
DATE 11-15-79 BY SP-5
RSG/MN

Re: Springfield letter and LHM to Bureau, 6/8/70

Enclosed for Albany Division are one copy each
of 2 photographs of subject showing him with and without sun-
glasses; and, one Xerox each of referenced letter and LHM.

On 6/12/70 ▓▓▓▓▓▓▓▓▓▓▓▓▓▓▓▓▓▓▓▓
State University of New York, Albany, New York,
telephonically contacted Springfield Division concerning status of
prosecution of subject in the Southern District of Illinois. ▓▓▓▓▓
▓▓▓ advised the State University of New York has retained
HUMPHREYS as an Associate Professor in the School of Criminal
Justice for the forthcoming Fall Term. The school has learned
of his involvement and federal charges against him concerning
damage to a Selective Service local board at Edwardsville, Ill.
▓▓▓▓▓▓ was tactfully referred to AUSA WILLIAM ROBERTS, SDI,
who is handling prosecution of HUMPHREYS.

For information of the Bureau and Albany, on 6/11/70
HUMPHREYS entered a plea of not guilty in U.S. District Court,
Southern District of Illinois, at Alton, Illinois before U.S.
District Judge OMER POOS. According to the bailiff, no trial date
has yet been set because Judge POOS is leaving shortly on his
vacation. The bailiff estimated the trial date would be set
some time in August or September, 1970.

It is anticipated subject's status as an Episcopal
priest and as a member of the faculty at Southern Illinois
University, Edwardsville, Illinois, will generate considerable
local publicity concerning federal charges against him arising

2: Bureau   (RM)
2: Albany (Enc.4)(RM)
3: Springfield (105-3118)
     (1: 52-2805)
DTS:vr
(7)

REC-82   EX 106
100- 459162 - 3

5 JUN 19 1970

INT. SEC.

SI 105-3118

from an event in which he led a group of students in an attack upon a Selective Service Local Board.

Albany is requested to advise if there is a source in a responsible position in State University of New York to whom copies of public source information of this nature could be furnished for the complete information of that University regarding the nature of HUMPHREYS. In the event Albany has such a source available, Springfield will submit recommendations of a COINTELPRO nature in a subsequent communication.

-2-

4

1 - Mr. Grubert

SAC, Springfield (105-3118)   6/30/70

ST-112   REC-138

Director, FBI (100-459062) - 3

ROBERT ALLAN LAUD HUMPHREYS
SM - MISC

Reurlets 6/8/70 and 6/17/70.

Inasmuch as the subject is an Episcopal priest as
well as a member of the faculty at Southern Illinois
University, Edwardsville, Illinois, you should limit
your investigative inquiries to reviewing files and
contacting established sources. Take no action which
could cause possible embarrassment to the Bureau.

Take no counterintelligence action against
subject without prior Bureau authority.

1 - Albany
HAG:rsm
(4)

ALL INFORMATION CONTAINED
HEREIN IS UNCLASSIFIED
DATE 11-15-79 BY SP-5
RJL/ML

NOTE:

Subject, who has been recommended for inclusion
in the Agitator Index, is currently out under $1500 bond
charged with violation Title 18, U.S. COde, Section 1361
and Title 50, Appendix, U.S. Code, Section 462 for an
assault on a Selective Service Board, Edwardsville, Illinois,
which occured 5/7/70. Subject plead not guilty to above
charges 6/11/70, U.S. District Court, Southern District of
Illinois. Subject reportedly has been retained as an
Associate Professor in the School of Criminal Justice for
the forthcoming Fall term at the State University of
New York, Albany, New York. Springfield is considering
a counterintelligence action against Humphreys in
connection with his forthcoming position at the State
University of New York.

MAILED 4 JUN 30 1970   COMM-FBI

Tolson
DeLoach
Walters
Mohr
Bishop
Casper
Callahan
Conrad
Felt
Gale
Rosen
Sullivan
Tavel   42
Soyars
Tele. Room
Holmes
Gandy   5 5 JUL 1 1970   TYPE UNIT

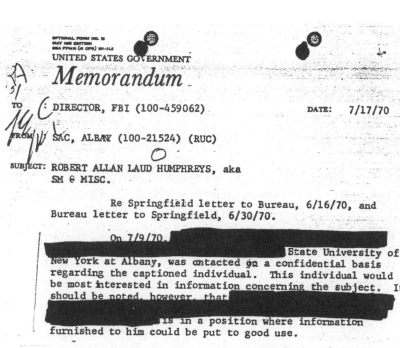

OPTIONAL FORM NO. 10
MAY 1962 EDITION
GSA FPMR (41 CFR) 101-11.6

UNITED STATES GOVERNMENT

Memorandum

TO : DIRECTOR, FBI (100-459062)   DATE: 7/17/70

FROM : SAC, ALBANY (100-21524) (RUC)

SUBJECT: ROBERT ALLAN LAUD HUMPHREYS, aka
SM & MISC.

Re Springfield letter to Bureau, 6/16/70, and
Bureau letter to Springfield, 6/30/70.

On 7/9/70, ▓▓▓▓▓▓▓▓▓▓▓▓▓▓▓▓ State University of   b7C
New York at Albany, was contacted on a confidential basis   b7D
regarding the captioned individual. This individual would
be most interested in information concerning the subject. It
should be noted, however, that ▓▓▓▓▓▓▓▓▓▓▓▓▓▓▓▓
▓▓▓▓▓▓▓▓▓▓▓▓▓▓▓▓ is in a position where information
furnished to him could be put to good use.

Further work in this particular case is being
left to the discretion of Bureau and Springfield. Albany
will make no further contacts at State University of New
York, regarding captioned subject UACB.

2- Bureau (RM)
2- Springfield (105-3118) (RM)
1- Albany
FJW:dap
(5)

ALL INFORMATION CONTAINED
HEREIN IS UNCLASSIFIED
DATE 11-15-79 BY SP-5 RTb/JHR

EX 106   100-459062-4

REC-33

1 JUL 20 1970

43   7339
55 JUL 28 1970   *Buy U.S. Savings Bonds Regularly on the Payroll Savings Plan*

OPTIONAL FORM NO. 10
MAY 1962 EDITION
GSA FPMR (41 CFR) 101-11.6

UNITED STATES GOVERNMENT

Memorandum

TO : DIRECTOR, FBI (100-459062)   DATE: 9/15/70

FROM : SAC, SPRINGFIELD (105-3118) (P)

SUBJECT: ROBERT ALLAN HUMPHREYS, aka   ALL INFORMATION CONTAINED
Laud Humphreys   HEREIN IS UNCLASSIFIED
SM - MISCELLANEOUS   DATE 11-15-79 BY Sp-5

Re Bureau letter to Springfield dated 6/30/70.

Enclosed herewith for the Bureau are the original
and ten copies of an LHM captioned as above, together with
two copies of an FD-376.

The LHM has been disseminated locally to USA, SDI,
Springfield; OSI, Chanute Air Force Base, Rantoul; NISO, Chi-
cago; Secret Service, Springfield; and MI Groups in Evanston,
Illinois and St. Louis, Missouri.

There is no characterization for the Youth International Party (YIP).

This LHM is being classified confidential to
protect sources of continuing value, the unauthorized
disclosure of which would be detrimental to the national
defense interests.

The sources mentioned in the enclosed LHM are
as follows:

b2
b7D

ENCLOSURE
2 - Bureau (100-459062) (Encls. 13) (RM)
3 - Springfield (105-3118)
        (66-1967)   REC-48   100-459062 - 5
RCH/vh   NOT RECORDED
(5)   ST-117   4 SEP 21 1970
        RAO 55

8 OCT 1 1970

FD-376 (Rev. 4-25-68)

UNITED STATES DEPARTMENT
FEDERAL BUREAU OF INVEST

In Reply, Please Refer to
File No.

WASHINGTON, D.C. 20535
September 15, 1970

Director
United States Secret Service
Department of the Treasury
Washington, D. C. 20220

Dear Sir:

The information furnished herewith concerns an individual who is believed to be covered by the agreement between the FBI and Secret Service concerning Presidential protection, and to fall within the category or categories checked.

1. ☐ Has attempted or threatened bodily harm to any government official or employee, including foreign government officials residing in or planning an imminent visit to the U. S., because of his official status.

2. ☐ Has attempted or threatened to redress a grievance against any public official by other than legal means.

3. ☐ Because of background is potentially dangerous; or has been identified as member or participant in communist movement; or has been under active investigation as member of other group or organization inimical to U. S.

4. ☐ U. S. citizens or residents who defect from the U. S. to countries in the Soviet or Chinese Communist blocs and return.

5. ☒ Subversives, ultrarightists, racists and fascists who meet one or more of the following criteria:

   (a) ☐ Evidence of emotional instability (including unstable residence and employment record) or irrational or suicidal behavior:
   (b) ☒ Expressions of strong or violent anti-U. S. sentiment;
   (c) ☒ Prior acts (including arrests or convictions) or conduct or statements indicating a propensity for violence and antipathy toward good order and government.

6. ☐ Individuals involved in illegal bombing or illegal bomb-making.

Photograph ☐ has been furnished ☐ enclosed ☐ is not available
☐ may be available through _____

Very truly yours,

DECLASSIFIED BY *Sp-5 RJb/kR*
ON *1-15-79*

John Edgar Hoover
Director

1 - Special Agent in Charge (Enclosure(s)
U. S. Secret Service

45

Enclosure(s)
(Upon removal of classified enclosures, if any, this transmittal form becomes UNCLASSIFIED.)

UNITED STATES DEPARTMENT OF JUSTICE **CONFIDENTIAL**

FEDERAL BUREAU OF INVESTIGATION

Springfield, Illinois
September 15, 1970

In Reply, Please Refer to
File No.

DECLASSIFIED BY SP-5 RJH/µL
ON 11-15-79

ROBERT ALLAN LAUD HUMPHREYS,
ALSO KNOWN AS
LAUD HUMPHREYS

███████████████████████████████████████ United b7C
States Attorney, Southern District of Illinois, Springfield,
advised on August 20, 1970 that the trial date set for
Robert Allan Laud Humphreys with regard to his indictment
for Destruction of Government Property and a violation of
the Selective Service Act has now been scheduled for December
2, 1970.

      According to records of the United States Attorney's
Office, Humphreys resides at 14 Biscayne Drive, Edwardsville,
Illinois, and he is currently unemployed, however, he is
scheduled to begin teaching as a professor at the State
University of New York, Albany, New York in the Fall of 1970.

      On ██████████████████████ who has furnished b2
reliable information in the past, advised that Professor b7D
Humphreys, who is well known to him, continues to reside at
14 Biscayne Drive, Edwardsville, Illinois, and he is unaware
of Humphreys' plans to travel to New York to assume a teaching
position at the State University of New York in Albany, New
York. He stated that Humphreys has not appeared on campus of
Southern Illinois University, Edwardsville, Illinois, since
the late Spring of 1970 and has made no official contact with
the University since that time.

      On ████████████████████ who has furnished reliable b2
information in the past, advised that Southern Illinois Univer- b7C
sity, Edwardsville, Illinois administrators had recognized
the Youth International Party (YIP) as an official campus
organization and that the YIP had listed its officers with
the Student Activities Office at Southern Illinois University,
Edwardsville for the school year 1969 - 1970. ████████ advised
that this listing indicated that the faculty advisor of the
YIP was listed as Laud Humphreys.

Excluded from automatic
downgrading and

      This document contains neither recommendations nor
conclusions of the FBI. It is the property of the FBI and is
loaned to your agency: it and its contents are not to be
distributed outside your agency. 100-459262

ENCLOSURE

CONFIDENTIAL

APPROPRIATE AGENCIES
AND FIELD OFFICES.
ADVISED BY ROUTING
SLIP(S) OF
DATE 1-21-09

46

-1*-

OPTIONAL FORM NO. 10
MAY 1962 EDITION
GSA FPMR (41 CFR) 101-11.6

UNITED STATES GOVERNMENT

Memorandum

TO : DIRECTOR, FBI (100-459062) DATE: October 26, 1970

FROM : SAC, SPRINGFIELD (105-3118) - P -

SUBJECT: ROBERT ALLAN LAUD HUMPHREYS, aka
Laud Humphreys
SM - MISCELLANEOUS

Re Springfield letter and letterhead memorandum to Bureau 9/15/70.

Subject is included in the Agitator Index of the Springfield Division. His most recent address was 14 Biscayne Drive, Edwardsville, Illinois, and he was employed as a professor in the Sociology Department at Southern Illinois University, Edwardsville (SIU-E).

On May 5, 1970, subject led approximately 100 students in a demonstration which began at SIU-E and ended in Local Draft Board 165-167, Edwardsville, during which the subject destroyed a photograph of President NIXON and a memorandum of the Selective Service System. He was subsequently charged with a violation of the Selective Service Act and with destruction of Government property and his trial in U.S. District Court, Southern District of Illinois, Springfield, Illinois, is scheduled to commence on December 2, 1970.

On October 20, 1970 ▓▓▓▓▓▓▓▓▓▓▓▓▓▓▓▓▓▓▓▓▓▓▓▓▓▓▓▓ advised that ROBERT ALLAN LAUD HUMPHREYS is now residing at 118 Main Street, Guilderland Center, New York, and he is teaching at the New York State University near that city.

LEADS:

ALL INFORMATION CONTAINED
HEREIN IS [UNCLASSIFIED]
DATE 11-15-79 BY Sp-5 RJG/WR

ALBANY DIVISION

At Guilderland Center, New York

Will verify subject's residence at 118 Main Street; will determine and verify his employment at New York State University and will notify the Bureau and Springfield upon verification.

REC-35

100-459062-6

2 - Bureau (100-459062) (RM)
2 - Albany (RM)
2 - Springfield (105-3118)

EX-103 17 OCT 29 1970

INT. SFC.

OPTIONAL FORM NO. 10
MAY 1962 EDITION
GSA FPMR (41 CFR) 101-11.6

UNITED STATES GOVERNMENT

Memorandum

TO : DIRECTOR, FBI (100-459062)   DATE: 11/17/70

FROM : SAC, ALBANY (100-21524) (RUC)

SUBJECT:
ROBERT ALLAN LAUD HUMPHREYS, aka
Laud Humphreys
SM - MISCELLANEOUS

Re Springfield letter to Bureau dated 10/26/70.

On 11/10/70 subject's residence, 118 Main
Street, Guilderland Center, New York, and his
employment, the State University of New York at Albany,
was verified.

This residence and employment was verified b7C
through contact with ███████████████████   b7D
University of New York at Albany.   State

In addition, ███████████ advised subject is
an Assistant Professor with a three year appointment
beginning September, 1970.

2-Bureau (RM)
2-Springfield (105-3118) (RM)
1-Albany
FJW:dml
(5)

ALL INFORMATION CONTAINED
HEREIN IS UNCLASSIFIED
DATE *11-15-79* BY *SP-5 RJ*

REC-48 *100 -459062 -7*

EX-113

8 NOV 19 1970

FD-128 (Rev. 5-7-70)
OPTIONAL FORM NO. 10
MAY 1962 EDITION
GSA GEN. REG. NO. 27

5010-104

UNITED STATES GOVERNMENT

Memorandum

TO : Director, FBI (Bufile - 100-459062)   DATE: 2/1/71

FROM : SAC SPRINGFIELD (105-3118)   Card UTD
Card sent 00
2-13-71

SUBJECT: ROBERT ALLAN HUMPHREYS, Aka.
Laud Humphreys
SM - MISCELLANEOUS

The captioned individual has been the subject of a security or racial investigation by this office. The
_____ALBANY_____ Division has verified the permanent presence of the subject in its division as
residing and working at the addresses listed below. The _____ALBANY_____ Division is being
considered the new office of origin.

Business Address, Name of Employing Concern and Address, Nature of Employment, and Union Affiliation, if any.	Residence address
Assistant Professor State University of New York Albany, New York	118 Main Street Guilderland Center New York, New York
Key Facility Data	ALL INFORMATION CONTAINED HEREIN IS UNCLASSIFIED DATE 11-15-79 BY sp-5
Geographical Reference Number _____	Responsibility _____

Check the following applicable statements:
[X] This individual is the subject of a [ ] Security Index Card [X] Agitator Index Card. [ ] Reserve Index Card.
(The Bureau is requested to make the appropriate changes in the [ ] Security Index [X] Agitator Index at the Seat
of Government. The _____ALBANY_____ Division should affix the addresses indicated above and
the appropriate case file number.)
[ ] This subject is tabbed Priority
[ ] This subject was carried as a Top Functionary.
[ ] Handwriting specimens have been furnished to the Bureau.
[ ] A photograph has been furnished to the Bureau.
[ ] Dissemination made Secret Service locally re above information.
[ ] A security flash notice has been placed on subject and a copy of this form is being designated for the Identification
Division for appropriate action.

The following pertinent items are being forwarded to the new Office of Origin with its copies of this letter:
[ ] Security Index Cards
[X] Agitator Index Card
[ ] Reserve Index Cards
[ ] Serials (specify)
[ ] Photograph of subject (check appropriate item listed below)
  [ ] Negative and three copies of most recent or best likeness photograph.
  [ ] None available.
  [X] Previously furnished.

(See page 2) REC 11   160 - 459062 - 8

RUC

17 FEB 8 1971

(2) Bureau (Registered Mail)
2 - Albany (enc. 11)
1 - Springfield (105-3118)   Enc. 11   (Registered Mail)
RCH:BLH (5)

54 FEB 22 1971

RESEARCH SECTION
NEW LEFT

SI 105-3118

ENCLOSURES FOR ALBANY:

Springfield airtel & LHM dated 1/19/70.

Springfield letter (FD-397) dated 6/8/70.

Springfield letter and LHM dated 6/8/70.

Springfield letter and LHM dated 9/15/70.

Three copies of SI rpt. of SA ████████████████ b7C
dated 2/1/71.

- 2 -

50

FD-263 (Rev. 12-19-67)

FEDERAL BUREAU OF INVESTIGATION

REPORTING OFFICE	OFFICE OF ORIGIN	DATE	INVESTIGATIVE PERIOD
SPRINGFIELD	ALBANY	2/1/71	11/10/70 – 1/7/71

TITLE OF CASE

ROBERT ALLAN LAUD HUMPHREYS, Aka.
Laud Humphreys

REPORT MADE BY

SA ▮▮▮▮▮▮▮▮ b7C   TYPED

CHARACTER OF CASE

SM – MISCELLANEOUS

REFERENCE   Albany let to Bureau 11/17/70.

– RUC –

ALL INFORMATION CONTAINED
HEREIN IS UNCLASSIFIED
DATE 11-15-79 BY sp-5 RJL/lR

ACCOMPLISHMENTS CLAIMED					☐ NONE	ACQUIT-TALS	CASE HAS BEEN:
CONVIC.	AUTO.	FUG.	FINES	SAVINGS	RECOVERIES		PENDING OVER ONE YEAR ☐YES ☐NO
							PENDING PROSECUTION
							OVER SIX MONTHS ☐YES ☐NO

APPROVED   SPECIAL AGENT IN CHARGE

COPIES MADE:

DO NOT WRITE IN SPACES BELOW

5 – Bureau (100–459062) (RM)
3 – Albany (100–21524) (RM)
1 – Springfield (105–3118)

100-459062 9   REC 1)

17 FEB 8 1971

ST-100

Dissemination Record of Attached Report					Notations
Agency	SS, RAO				
Request Recd.					
Date Fwd.	2/12/71				NEW LEFT)
How Fwd.	FD-376, 0-C				
By	JHK/lcp				

51   6 OFEB 17 1971   A*
                          COVER PAGE   GPO : 1968 O - 299-885

FD-204 (Rev. 3-3-59)

UNITED STATES DEPARTMENT OF JUSTICE
FEDERAL BUREAU OF INVESTIGATION

Copy to:

Report of: SA ▓▓▓▓▓▓▓▓▓▓ *b7c*
Date: February 1, 1971

Office: SPRINGFIELD

Field Office File #: SI 105-3118

Bureau File #: 100-459062

Title: ROBERT ALLAN LAUD HUMPHREYS

Character: SECURITY MATTER - MISCELLANEOUS

ALL INFORMATION CONTAINED
HEREIN IS ░░░░░░░ IED
DATE *11-15-79* BY *sp-5 RJH/jR*

Synopsis: Subject resides 118 Main Street, Guilderland Center, New York; employed as Assistant Professor at State University of New York, Albany. On 1/7/71 subject sentenced to custody of Attorney General for term of one year; the first four months to be spent in jail type institution with the balance suspended and subject placed on three years probation. Sentence imposed for violation of Title 18, Section 1361, U.S. Code.

- RUC -

DETAILS: RESIDENCE AND EMPLOYMENT

On November 10, 1970 subject's residence, 118 Main Street, Guilderland Center, New York and his employment, the State University of New York at Albany, was verified.

b7c
b7D

This residence and employment was verified through contact with ▓▓▓▓▓▓▓▓▓▓▓▓▓▓ State University of New York at Albany.

In addition, ▓▓▓▓▓▓▓▓ advised subject is an Assistant Professor with a three year appointment beginning September, 1970.

52

U. S. GOVERNMENT PRINTING OFFICE : 1949 O - 351-878

SI 105-3118

MISCELLANEOUS ACTIVITIES

On January 7, 1971 subject appeared in U.S. District Court, Southern District of Illinois, Springfield, Illinois, before Judge OMER POOS, after originally entering a plea of guilty on December 3, 1970 to a violation of Title 18, U.S. Code, Section 1361. At the time of his appearance on January 7, 1971 the subject was sentenced by Judge POOS to the custody of the Attorney General for a term of one year; the first four months of which were to be spent in a jail type institution with the balance suspended and subject was placed on probation for a period of three years.

FD-397 (Rev. 2-20-69)

UNITED STATES GOVERNMENT

Memorandum

TO : Director, FBI (Bufile- 100-459062)   DATE: 3/19/71

FROM : SAC. ALBANY (100-21524)

Card UID
Card sent OO
4-1-71

SUBJECT: ROBERT ALLAN HUMPHREYS, aka
Laud Humphreys; SM - MISCELLANEOUS

AGITATOR INDEX

☐ Add Subject to Index   ☒ Change Index Card   ☐ Delete Subject

Name	FBI Number

Aliases

Citizenship
☐ Native Born   ☐ Naturalized   ☐ Alien

Subject also on	Race	Sex
☐ SI ☐ RI		☐ Male ☐ Female

Organizational Affiliation

☐ 01 ANP	☐ 07 KLAN	☐ 12 PLP	☐ 17 SNCC
☐ 02 AVN	☐ 08 LA	☐ 13 PRN	☐ 18 SWP
☐ 03 BNAT	☐ 09 MIN	☐ 14 RAM	☐ 19 WWP
☐ 04 BPP	☐ 10 NOI	☐ 15 SCLC	☐ 99 MISC
☐ 05 COM	☐ 11 NSRP	☐ 16 SDS	(Specify)
☐ 06 CORE			

Date of Birth	Place of Birth

Position in Organization	Occupation, Business Address (Show Name of Employing Concern)

ALL INFORMATION CONTAINED
HEREIN IS UNCLASSIFIED
DATE 11-15-79 BY Sp-5 / 100 - 459062 -
RJG/mc

Residence Address

118 Main Street, Guilderland Center, New York.

REGISTERED MAIL

2-Bureau
1-Albany
FJW:lal 7227
(3) OC MAY 3 1971

NOT RECORDED

12 MAR 26 1971

54

FD-366 (5-6-64)

UNITED STATES DEPARTMENT OF JUSTICE
FEDERAL BUREAU OF INVESTIGATION

In Reply, Please Refer to
File No.

Albany, New York
March 19, 1971

SUBJECT: ROBERT ALLAN LAUD HUMPHREYS

REFERENCE: Springfield report of SA ▮▮▮▮▮▮▮▮▮▮ b7C
             dated February 1, 1971.

Referenced communication contained subject's residence and/or employment address. A recent change has been determined and is being set forth below (change only specified):

Residence: 118 Main Street, Guilderland Center,
             New York, New York

Employment:

100- 459062

100 - 459062
NOT RECORDED
8 APR 30 1971

Copy to SS
by routing slip for
Info   action
date 4/29/71
by JHK/cws

SS 31 MAY 3 1971

OPTIONAL FORM NO. 10
MAY 1962 EDITION
GSA FPMR (41 CFR) 101-11.6

UNITED STATES GOVERNMENT

Memorandum

TO : DIRECTOR, FBI (100-459062)　　　　　DATE: 3/31/71

FROM : SAC, ALBANY (100-21524) (C)

SUBJECT: ROBERT ALLAN HUMPHREYS, aka
Laud Humphreys;
SM-MISCELLANEOUS
(OO: ALBANY)

　　　　　Re Albany FD-397 dated 3/19/71.

　　　　　A review of subject's file fails to reflect
a need for additional investigation at this time.

　　　　　This matter is being closed by the Albany Division
subject to reopening for periodic review and verifications.

　2-Bureau (RM)
　1-Albany
　FJW:dml
　(3)

ALL INFORMATION CONTAINED
HEREIN IS ... .IED
DATE 1-15-79 BY SP-5 RJH/jc

EX 101

REC-15 /00-459062-10

1 APR 5 1971

NEW LEFT

E,2.8
54 APR 29 1971

56

FBI

Date: 2-2-66

Transmit the following in _____
(Type in plaintext or code)

Via AIRTEL AIRMAIL _____
(Priority)

TO: DIRECTOR, FBI

FROM: SAC, ST. LOUIS (173-new) P

RE: UNSUB;
CHANAULT's RESTAURANT
MEMPHIS, TENN.,
9-12-65
ROBERT A. LAUD HUMPHREYS - VICTIM
PUBLIC ACCOMMODATIONS
CRA, 1964
OO: MEMPHIS

On 2-1-66, Rev. ROBERT A. LAUD HUMPHREYS, Ordained
Episcopal Minister, now in graduate school, Washington University,
SLMO, in signed statement said at 7:40 P. M., Sunday, 9-12-65,
he stopped at CHANAULT's RESTAURANT, Bellevue St. at Quinn,
Memphis, Tenn., for dinner. He was in clerical dress and was
accompanied by MRS. CONSTANCE WITTE, SLMO, wife of Episcopal
Minister; MR. WILLIAM MATHEWS, SLMO; and Rev. ROBERT MAYO,
Episcopal Minister, SLMO. All are white except MAYO, a negro.
After the group had been seated in a booth about 15 minutes, the
restaurant manager, a white man in late 40's, about 5'8"-10",
220 - 230 #, called HUMPHREYS away from the others and told him
they served both white and negroes, but not as mixed group
and refused them service.

Preliminary investigation being initiated.

THE MEMPHIS OFFICE:
1. Interview proprietor of CHANAULT's RESTAURANT.
2. Determine full name and residence of owner and
manager of CHANAULT's RESTAURANT.

THE ST. LOUIS OFFICE:
1. Will interview appropriate witnesses in SLMO.

3 - Bureau,   2 - Memphis
   St. Louis
CPB:wma
(6)
Approved: _____   Sent _____ M _____
         Special Agent in Charge

FEDERAL BUREAU OF INVESTIGATION

REPORTING OFFICE	OFFICE OF ORIGIN	DATE	INVESTIGATIVE PERIOD
ST. LOUIS	MEMPHIS	2/4/66	2/1 - 3/66

TITLE OF CASE		

REPORT MADE BY	TYPED
SA C. PERSHING BELL	bam

UNSUB;
Chanault's Restaurant
Memphis, Tennessee,
9/12/65
ROBERT A. LAUD HUMPHREYS -
VICTIM

CHARACTER OF CASE

PUBLIC ACCOMMODATIONS
CRA, 1964

REFERENCE: St. Louis airtel to the Director, dated 2/2/66.

STATUS: - RUC -

LEAD:

THE MEMPHIS DIVISION

AT MEMPHIS, TENNESSEE

As set out in re airtel to Bureau, 2/2/66, will interview proprietor of Chanault's Restaurant, Bellevue St., at Quinn, and will determine full name and residence of owner and manager of Chanault's Restaurant.

- A* -

COVER PAGE

APPROVED	SPECIAL AGENT IN CHARGE	DO NOT WRITE IN SPACES BELOW

COPIES MADE:

2 - Bureau

3 - Memphis
   (1 - USA, Memphis)

1 - St. Louis (173-57)

$173-2851-2$

2 FEB 7 1966

Dissemination Record of Attached Report				Notations
Agency	CRD			
Request Recd.				
Date Fwd.				
How Fwd.				
By				

SIX
STAT. SECT.

58

UNI 🖰 STATES DEPAR TMENT OF J 🖰 ICE
FEDERAL BUREAU OF INVESTIGATION

Copy to: 1 - U. S. Attorney, Memphis

Report of: SA C. PERSHING BELL   **Office:**   ST. LOUIS
Date: February 4, 1966

Field Office File #: SL 173-57   **Bureau File #:**

Title: UNKNOWN SUBJECT;
               Chanault's Restaurant
               Memphis, Tennessee,
               September 12, 1965
               ROBERT A. LAUD HUMPHREYS - VICTIM
Character:

               PUBLIC ACCOMMODATIONS
               CIVIL RIGHTS ACT, 1964
Synopsis:

               Rev. ROBERT A. LAUD HUMPHREYS, Rev. ROBERT MAYO,
               Episcopal Ministers, Mrs. CONSTANCE WITTE, wife
               of an Episcopal Minister, and Mr. WILLIAM MATHEUS
               returning to SLMO by auto from Annual National
               Meeting, Episcopal Society for Cultural and Racial
               Unity, Jackson, Miss., on 9/12/65, stopped at
               Chanault's Restaurant, Bellevue St., at Quinn,
               Memphis, Tenn., about 7:40 PM for dinner. Rev. MAYO
               is a Negro, the others in the party caucasian.
               Rev. HUMPHREYS, only one in clerical dress, was
               called aside by restaurant manager who refused
               to serve them as racially mixed group. Said the
               restaurant served both Negroes and white customers,
               but had to by served at separate tables.

                          - RUC -

DETAILS: AT ST. LOUIS, MISSOURI

          This investigation is predicated on the following
information furnished by Reverend ROBERT A. LAUD HUMPHREYS,
8316 Correll Avenue, on February 1, 1966.

4-750 (2-7-79)

FEDERAL BUREAU OF INVESTIGATION
FOIPA DELETED PAGE INFORMATION SHEET

___9___ Page(s) withheld entirely at this location in the file. One or more of the following statements, whi indicated, explain this deletion.

[X] Deleted under exemption(s) ___(K)(2)___ with no segregable material available for release to you.

[ ] Information pertained only to a third party with no reference to you or the subject of your request.

[ ] Information pertained only to a third party. Your name is listed in the title only.

[ ] Document(s) originating with the following government agency(ies) _____ _____ , was/were forwarded to them for direct response to

_____ Page(s) referred for consultation to the following government agency(ies); _____ _____ as the information originated with them. You will be advised of availability upon return of the material to the FBI.

_____ Page(s) withheld for the following reason(s):

_____

_____

[ ] For your information: _____

_____

[ ] The following number is to be used for reference regarding these pages:

_____

XXXXXXXXXXXXXXXX
DELETED PAGE(S
NO DUPLICATION F
FOR THIS PAGE
XXXXXXXXXXXXXXXX

XXXXXX
XXXXXX
XXXXXX

FEDERAL BUREAU OF INVESTIGATION

Date _____ 2/4/66

1

Reverend ROBERT A. LAUD HUMPHREYS, 8318 Cornell Avenue, was interviewed and furnished the following signed statement:

"St. Louis, Mo.
February 1, 1966

"I, R. A. Laud Humphreys, make the following free and voluntary statement to C. Pershing Bell and Albert J. Rushing, who have identified themselves to me as Special Agents of the Federal Bureau of Investigation.

"I am an ordained Minister of the Episcopal Church but am presently doing graduate work in Sociology at Washington University.

"In September, 1965, I attended a meeting in Jackson, Mississippi, of the Episcopal Society for Cultural and Racial Unity. Accompanied by William Matheus, Mrs. Constance Witte and Reverend Robert Mayo, I left Jackson on Sunday afternoon, September 12, 1965 to return to St. Louis. We were traveling in my car and stopped in Memphis, Tennessee to have the car serviced. We asked the attendant at the service station where we could get dinner and he recommended Chanault's Restaurant which was located next door to the service station. Chanault's is located on Bellevue Street near Quinn, in Memphis and is on highway 51. We had been traveling on Interstate highway 55.

"Reverend Mayo is a Negro and when we entered the restaurant the four of us took seats together in a booth. The other three of us are white. I noticed that there were Negroes being served in the restaurant as well as white people. We arrived at 7:40 p.m. and visited the rest rooms. I noticed that the restaurant

- 2 -

On ___2/1/66___ at ___St. Louis, Missouri___ File # ___SL 173-___ 57

SA ALBERT J. RUSHING,
SA C. PERSHING BELL : mja

by _____ Date dictated ___2/2/66___

60

2
SL 173- 57

"was crowded and after about fifteen minutes
nobody had come to take our order. I thought
perhaps it was because the place was crowded
until it was called to my attention that the
manager of the restaurant was trying to
attract my attention. I noticed the manager
motioning to me and got up to see what he
wanted. I talked to him about twelve or
fifteen feet from the others in my group.
The manager told me that he could not serve my
group and said, 'You understand why.' I told
him I did not understand and he said they served
Negroes but did not serve mixed groups. I told
him this was illegal and he said it was not,
that they did serve Negroes but did not serve
mixed groups. We were both courteous and polite
during our discussion.

"Following the discussion I went to the
rest room while the other members of my group
waited on me and as soon as I rejoined them,
we left the restaurant without being served.

"I have read this three-page statement and
acknowledge it to be an accurate report of the
occurrence in Memphis, Tennessee, last September12th.

"/s/ Robert A. Laud Humphreys

"Witnessed:

"/s/ Albert J. Rushing, Special Agent, FBI, 2/1/66

"/s/ C. Pershing Bell, Special Agent, FBI, 2/1/66."

In addition to the information contained in the
above signed statement, Reverend HUMPHREYS advised that he is
presently earning his livlihood as a Research Assistnat for the
Medical Care Research Center, 216 South Kingshighway,
St. Louis, Missouri. With regard to the above incident, he said

- 3 -

61

shortly after he returned to St. Louis he reported it to the
National Association for the Advancement of Colored People, but
did not know whether any further action had been taken. He said
WILLIAM MATHEUS is a lay assistant at St. Stephen's Episcopal
Church, 14th and Park, St. Louis, Missouri, that Mrs. CONSTANCE
WITTE is the wife of Reverend WALTER WITTE, who is pastor of the
St. Stephen's Episcopal Church, and Mrs. WITTE lives at 3124
Longfellow. He said Reverend ROBERT MAYO is an Episcopal
Minister at the Near Northside Team Ministry, 2231 Dixon,
St. Louis, Missouri.

Reverend HUMPHREYS said he felt certain that the
reason the manager of the Chanault's Restaurant singled him
(HUMPHREYS) out for discussion of this matter was due to the
fact that he (HUMPHREYS) was the only one of the group wearing
his clerical dress. He said none of the other members of the
group overheard the conversation he had with the manager,
but as soon as it was completed he returned and told the others
what had been said. He said he felt certain that the individual
he was talking to was the owner as well as the manager and that
his name might have been CHANAULT, but he could not be certain
of this. He described this individual as follows:

Race	White
Sex	Male
Age	Late 40s
Height	5'9" or 10"
Weight	220 - 230 pounds
Build	Quite heavy and stocky
Hair	Graying.

He said he was certain he could identify this man
if he saw him again. Reverend ROBERT A. LAUD HUMPHREYS is
described as follows:

Race	White
Sex	Male
Date of Birth	October 16, 1930
Place of Birth	Chickashaw, Oklahoma
Height	5'9½"
Weight	160 pounds
Eyes	Brown
Hair	Dark Brown
Complexion	Medium
Build	Medium
Residence	8318 Cornell Avenue.

- 4 -

FEDERAL BUREAU OF INVESTIGATION

REPORTING OFFICE	OFFICE OF ORIGIN	DATE	INVESTIGATIVE PERIOD	
MEMPHIS	MEMPHIS	2/9/66	2/7-8/66	
TITLE OF CASE		REPORT MADE BY		TYPED
CHANGED REGINALD VINCENT CHENAULT; Chenault's Restaurant, Memphis, Tenn., 9/12/65; ROBERT A. LAUD HUMPHREYS - VICTIM		SA MERRILL E. MC CLOUGHAN		ngn
		CHARACTER OF CASE		
		PA - CRA, 1964		

Title is marked changed to reflect subject's name
and correct spelling of restaurant name, formerly carried
as "UNSUB; CHANAULT's RESTAURANT, MEMPHIS, TENN., 9/12/65;
ROBERT A. LAUD HUMPHREYS - VICTIM; PA - CRA, 1964."

REFERENCES:

        St. Louis airtel to Director dated 2/2/66.
        Report of SA C. PERSHING BELL dated 2/4/66 at
        St. Louis.

- C -

A*
COVER PAGE

Case has been: Pending over one year ☐ Yes ☐ No; Pending prosecution over six months ☐ Yes ☐ No				
APPROVED		SPECIAL AGENT IN CHARGE	DO NOT WRITE IN SPACES BELOW	
COPIES MADE:				MCT-41
2 - Bureau 1 - USA, Memphis 1 - Memphis (173-161)			*173-* 2851-3	REC 1
Xerox Synopsis			16 FEB 11 1966	

Dissemination Record of Attached Report			Notations	
Agency	CRD			
Request Recd.				
Date Fwd.	2/11/66			
How Fwd.	634C			
By	mrs/jah			

63   00 FEB 18 1966

UNITED STATES DEPARTMENT OF JUSTICE
FEDERAL BUREAU OF INVESTIGATION

Copy to: 1 - USA, Memphis

Report of: SA MERRILL E. MC CLOUGHAN   Office: MEMPHIS
Date: February 9, 1966

Field Office File #: ME 173-161   Bureau File #:

Title: REGINALD VINCENT CHENAULT;
Chenault's Restaurant,
Memphis, Tennessee, September 12, 1965;
ROBERT A. LAUD HUMPHREYS - VICTIM

Character: PUBLIC ACCOMMODATIONS
CIVIL RIGHTS ACT OF 1964

Synopsis: Subject, who is manager and co-owner of Chenault's Restaurant, interviewed. States he recalls incident of several months ago and did speak to victim, partner not on premises at time, and he does not know name of victim. Subject told victim if Negro in their party would sit at another table they would all be served. Said several customers complained to him at the time about white woman sitting next to Negro man, and subject then spoke to victim for the protection of the victim and his party, as well as subject's business. Subject states policy of Chenault's Restaurant is to serve both Negroes and whites as well as mixed groups; however, if necessary, for protection of customers as well as business, the management will specify seating arrangements of customers. Restaurant is partnership, owned by subject and wife, WILLIE MAE CHENAULT, who both reside at 4516 Ernie Drive, Whitehaven, Tenn.

- C -

DETAILS:

     This investigation was initiated upon receipt of a complaint by the St. Louis Office of the Federal Bureau of Investigation. This complaint was received on February 1, 1966, from Reverend ROBERT A. LAUD HUMPHREYS, ordained Episcopal minister, now in graduate school, Washington University, St. Louis, Missouri, in a signed statement which revealed that at 7:40 p.m., Sunday, September 12, 1965,

64

ME 173-161

he stopped at Chenault's Restaurant, Bellevue Street
at Quinn, Memphis, Tennessee, for dinner. He was in
clerical dress and was accompanied by Mrs. CONSTANCE WITTE,
wife of an Episcopal minister; Mr. WILLIAM MATHEWS; and
Reverend ROBERT MAYO, Episcopal minister. All the individuals,
according to the complaint, are white with the exception
of Reverend MAYO, a Negro. He said that after the group
had been seated in a booth about fifteen minutes, the
restaurant manager, a white man, called HUMPHREYS away
from the others and told him that the restaurant served
both whites and Negroes, but not as a mixed group, and
refused them service.

2

65

4-750 (2-7-79)

FEDERAL BUREAU OF INVESTIGATION
FOIPA DELETED PAGE INFORMATION SHEET

___2___ Page(s) withheld entirely at this location in the file. One or more of the following statements, wh indicated, explain this deletion.

☒ Deleted under exemption(s) _(K)(2)_ _____ with no segregabl material available for release to you.

☐ Information pertained only to a third party with no reference to you or the subject of your request.

☐ Information pertained only to a third party. Your name is listed in the title only.

☐ Document(s) originating with the following government agency(ies) _____
_____ , was/were forwarded to them for direct response to

_____ Page(s) referred for consultation to the following government agency(ies); _____
_____ as the information originated with them. You will
be advised of availability upon return of the material to the FBI.

_____ Page(s) withheld for the following reason(s):

_____
_____
_____

☐ For your information: _____

☐ The following number is to be used for reference regarding these pages: _____
_____

XXXXXXXXXXXXXXXX
DELETED PAGE(S
NO DUPLICATION F
FOR THIS PAGE
XXXXXXXXXXXXXX

XXXXXX
XXXXXX
X XXXXXX

Appendix C

Poster from the Washington University Bulletin Board

O R A L ' S   B E S T I A R Y :

(PHYLUM OF BLEAK HYPOTHESES)

<u>Inter</u> <u>Alios</u> <u>Platonicus</u>, or Silver-Tongued High-Priestly Bird.

Given to nesting in high places, this raptorial bird may soar to
great heights before diving to feed on carrion. A completely carnivorous
creature, he seeks his prey among underdogs and those who flock with
them, as well as among the dead. His feeding habits include a distinct
preference for personalities. He chews on thoughts only when personalities
are not available. While devouring his prey, his song is said to be
quite eloquent.

When perched on the pinnacles of the Temple, he has been heard
to cry: "I thank God I am not as other birds are, living on grants and
engaging in research with living subjects." This longer refrain is
often punctuated by short cries such as: "I have moral character!"
"I am a radical!"

WARNING: The Silver-Tongued High-Priestly Bird is <u>not</u> to be
confused with his cousin, the Silver-Winged Grant-Snatcher. Although
these birds have much in common, the former is vicious (having an "erect"
style) and the latter is mild-mannered (having a "flaccid" style).

Appendix D

Systematic Observation Sheet

SYSTEMATIC OBSERVATION SHEET   DATE: 3/24/67 DAY: _Friday_

O = Observer (1) (2) General Conditions: Weather & temp. _Beautiful, clear day,_ T 85°
X = Principal Aggressor   # & type of people in parks: _moderate, mostly_
                                        families + youngsters enjoying school holiday
Y = Principal Passive Participant   est. volume of gay activity:
                                        very little
A - N = Other Participants   Place: C-1   F-1   O-1   T-1
Z = Law Enforcement Personnel   C-2   F-2   O-2   T-2
                                                     F-3
Time Began: _2:30 p.m._   F-4
Time Ended: _2:45 p.m._   F-5

Participants: [include symbol, sex, age,
              attire, other distinguishing
              characteristics, type of auto
              driven]

X: _28, orange T-shirt, tan slacks, driving_
yellow Chev. Convertible '67, Ill. license

Y: _23, white T-shirt + jeans, driving_
older Falcon

Others: _____

_____

_____

_____

F = Fellatio performed
C = Contact made

Description of Action: [note: when possible, indicate: delays in autos, etc., before
    entering research...manner of approaches...types of sexual roles taken...
    nature of interceptions and reaction to them...ANYTHING WHICH MAY BE SPOKEN...
    any masturbation going on...actions of lookout(s)...REACTION TO TEENAGERS
    AND ANY PARTICIPATION BY THEM...reactions to observer...length of time of
    sexual acts...spitting, washing of hands, wiping, etc.]

O drove up behind yellow conv. White Falcon already there. O enters Tearoom
& takes position. 2 min. later, X enters, eyes O. 2 more min., Y
enters, eye contact between X and Y. X looks at O, who nods, X
makes hand contact with Y. Both move to far stall, engage in
F, X active, Y passive. After act X clears throat in other
stall. Y leaves, O following shortly.

Appendix E

Data Sources and Methods

Existing Records: One Institute and Archives in Los Angeles; Pitzer College Archives in Claremont, California; Archives of the Episcopal Church in New York City; transcriptions of Laud Humphreys's Federal Trial and Appeal; and Laud Humphreys's FBI file released under the Freedom of Information Act.

Primary Data: These sources included phone interviews and e-mail letters, both accumulated through snowball sampling techniques. This was pursued until no new personal contacts could be elicited.

The Interchange of Primary and Secondary Data: At times it was necessary to work back and forth between interviews and existing records. In some cases previously unknown sources of existing records were mentioned during an interview, and in other instances existing records revealed the names of possible informants.

References

Amburn, Ellis. 1980. Letter to Theron Raines, August 14. One Institute and Archives.

Anderson, Nels. 1923. *The Hobo: The Sociology of the Homeless Man.* Chicago: University of Chicago Press.

Bannister, Robert C. 1987. *Sociology and Scientism: The American Quest for Objectivity, 1880–1940.* Chapel Hill: University of North Carolina Press.

———. 1991. *Jessie Bernard: The Making of a Feminist.* New Brunswick, N.J.: Rutgers University Press.

Basinger, Julianne. 1997. "Award Causes Mild Protest at Annual Sociology Meeting." *Chronicle of Higher Education,* August 12.

Beauchamp, Tom L., Ruth R. Faden, R. Jay Wallace Jr., and Leroy Walters. 1982. *Ethical Issues in Social Research.* Baltimore, Md.: The Johns Hopkins University Press.

Becker, Howard S. 1963. *Outsiders: Studies in the Sociology of Deviance.* New York: Free Press.

Bellah, Robert N., Richard Madsen, William M. Sullivan, Ann Swidler, Steven M. Tipton. 1985. *Habits of the Heart: Individualism and Commitment in American Life.* New York: Harper and Row.

Beller, Clair Humphreys. 2001. Letter to John F. Galliher, n.d. (mailed May 21).

Berg, Bruce L. 1995. *Qualitative Research Methods for the Social Sciences.* 2nd ed. Boston: Allyn and Bacon.

Blumer, Herbert. 1955. "Attitudes and the Social Act." *Social Problems* 3:59–65.

Blumstein, Philip W., and Pepper Schwartz. 1976. "Bisexuality in Men." *Urban Life* 5:339–58.

Bramel, Dana. 1962. "A Dissonance Theory Approach to Defensive Projection." *Journal of Abnormal and Social Psychology* 64:121–29.

Brekhus, Wayne. 2003. *Peacocks, Chameleons, Centaurs: Gay Suburbia and the Grammar of Social Identity.* Chicago: University of Chicago Press.

Brown, Irene. 1968. Letter to Executive Vice Chancellor George Pake, June 21. One Institute and Archives.

Cahill, Spencer E., with W. Distler, C. Lachowetz, A. Meaney, R. Tarallo, and T. Willard. 1985. "Meanwhile Backstage: Public Bathrooms and the Interaction Order." *Urban Life* 14:33–58.

Carrier, Joseph. 1999. "Reflections on Ethical Problems Encountered in Field

Research on Mexican Male Homosexuality." *Culture, Health, and Sexuality* 1:207–21.

———. 2001. Interview with John F. Galliher, April 14.

Cassell, Joan. 1982. "Harms, Benefits, Wrongs, and Rights in Fieldwork." In *The Ethics of Social Research: Fieldwork, Regulation, and Publication*, ed. Joan E. Sieber, 7–31 (New York: Springer-Verlag).

Chambliss, William J. 1978. *On the Take: From Petty Crooks to Presidents*. Bloomington: Indiana University Press.

Chapoulie, Jean-Michel. 1987. "Everett C. Hughes and the Development of Fieldwork in Sociology." *Urban Life* 15:259–98.

Chauncey, George. 2000. "The Queer History and Politics of Lesbian and Gay Studies." In *Queer Frontiers: Millennial Geographies, Genders, and Generations*, ed. Joseph A. Boone, M. Dupius, M. Meeker, K. Quimby, C. Sarver, D. Silverman, and R. Weatherston, 298–315 (Madison: University of Wisconsin Press).

Claremont Courier. 1988. Laud Humpreys [Obituary], September 14, 12.

Clark, Jon, Celia Modgil, and Sohan Modgil, eds. 1990. *Robert K. Merton: Consensus and Controversy*. London: Falmer.

Clark, Jon, ed. 1996. *James S. Coleman*. London: Falmer.

Clawson, Dan, and Robert Zussman. 1998. "Canon and Anti-canon for a Fragmented Discipline." In *Required Reading: Sociology's Most Influential Books*, ed. Dan Clawson, 3–17 (Amherst: University of Massachusetts Press).

Cohen, Fred. 1971. Review of *Tearoom Trade*. *Criminal Law Bulletin* 7:67–69.

Corzine, Jay, and Richard Kirby. 1977. "Cruising the Truckers: Sexual Encounters in a Highway Rest Area." *Urban Life* 6:171–92.

Coser, Lewis A. 1959. "Participant Observation and the Military: An Exchange." *American Sociological Review* 24:397–98.

———. 1971. *Masters of Sociological Thought: Ideas in Historical and Social Context*. New York: Harcourt Brace Jovanovich.

Cowan, Rex. 1970. "Loo View" [review of *Tearoom Trade*]. *Hamstead and Highgate Express*, November 6. One Institute and Archives.

Daily Oklahoman. 1953. "State Legislator Dies in Chickasha," November 19, 1.

Davis, John Paul. 1970. Letter to Judge Omer Poos, November 17. One Institute and Archives.

Deegan, Mary Jo. 1988. *Jane Addams and the Men of the Chicago School, 1892–1918*. Chicago: University of Chicago Press.

Dentler, Robert A., and Kai T. Erikson. 1959. "The Functions of Deviance in Groups." *Social Problems* 7:98–107.

Denzin, Norman K., and Yvonna S. Lincoln, eds. 1994. *Handbook of Qualitative Research*. Thousand Oaks, Calif.: Sage.

Desroches, Frederick J. 1990. "Tearoom Trade: A Research Update." *Qualitative Sociology* 13:39–61.

Deutscher, Irwin. 1966. "Words and Deeds: Social Science and Social Policy." *Social Problems* 13:235–54.

————. 1973. *What We Say/What We Do: Sentiments and Acts.* Glenview, Ill.: Scott, Foresman.

Deutscher, Irwin, and Verda M. Deutscher. 1955. "Cohesion in a Small Group—A Case Study." *Social Forces* 38:336–41.

Donnelly, Peter. 1981. "Running the Gauntlet: The Moral Order of Pornographic Movie Theaters." *Urban Life* 10:239–64.

Dooley, David. 1995. *Social Research Methods.* 3rd ed. Upper Saddle River, N.J.: Prentice Hall.

Doyle, Patrick. 1973. Review of *Out of the Closets. The Advocate,* March 14, 40.

Duberman, Martin. 1993. *Stonewall.* New York: Penguin.

Durkheim, Emile. 1964. *The Division of Labor in Society.* New York: Free Press.

Dworkin, Gerald. 1982. "Must Subjects Be Objects?" In *Ethical Issues in Social Science Research,* ed. Tom L. Beauchamp, Ruth R. Faden, R. Jay Wallace Jr., and Leroy Walters, 246–54 (Baltimore, Md.: The Johns Hopkins University Press).

Eiselein, E. B. 1971. Review of *Tearoom Trade. American Anthropologist* 73:860.

Eliot, Thomas H. 1968a. Letter to Laud Humphreys, June 18. One Institute and Archives.

————. 1968b. Letter to Laud Humphreys, July 1. One Institute and Archives.

————. 1968c. Letter to Alex Morin, July 1. One Institute and Archives.

Episcopal Clerical Directory. 1999. Episcopal Church Archives, New York, N.Y.

Escoffier, Jeffrey. 1992. "Generations and Paradigms: Mainstreams in Lesbian and Gay Studies." *Journal of Homosexuality* 24:7–26.

Federal Bureau of Investigation File. 2001. Laud Humphreys. Released July 20.

Fine, Gary A. 1993. "Ten Lies of Ethnography: Moral Dilemmas of Field Research." *Journal of Contemporary Ethnography* 22:267–94.

French, J. P. R. 1944. "Organized and Unorganized Groups under Fear and Frustration." *Iowa Studies in Child Welfare* 20:231–308.

Galliher, John F. 1973. "The Protection of Human Subjects: A Reexamination of the Professional Code of Ethics." *American Sociologist* 8:93–100.

Galliher, John F., and James M. Galliher. 1995. *Marginality and Dissent in Twentieth-Century American Sociology.* Albany: State University of New York Press.

Gamson, Joshua. 2000. "Sexualities, Queer Theory, and Qualitative Research." In *Handbook of Qualitative Research,* ed. Norman K. Denzin and Yvonna S. Lincoln, 2nd ed., 347–65 (Thousand Oaks, Calif.: Sage).

Gans, Herbert J. 1970. Letter to the Honorable Omer Poos, December 15. One Institute and Archives.

Gerhardt, Ita, ed. 1993. *Talcott Parsons on National Socialism.* New York: Aldine De Gruyter.

Glazer, Myron. 1975. "Impersonal Sex." In Laud Humphreys, *Tearoom Trade: Impersonal Sex in Public Places,* Retrospect: 213–22 (Chicago: Aldine).

Glick, Brian. 1989. *War at Home: Covert Action against U.S. Activists and What We Can Do about It.* Boston: South End.

Goffman, Erving. 1963. *Stigma: Notes on the Management of Spoiled Identity.* Englewood Cliffs, N.J.: Prentice Hall.

Goodwin, Glenn A., Irving Louis Horowitz, and Peter M. Nardi. 1991. "Laud Humphreys: A Pioneer in the Practice of Social Science." *Sociological Inquiry* 61:139–47.

Goodwin, Glenn A., and Laud Humphreys. 1982. "Freeze Dried Stigma: Cybernetics and Social Control." *Humanity and Society* 6:391–408.

Gouldner, Alvin W. 1968. "The Sociologist as Partisan: Sociology and the Welfare State." *American Sociologist* 3:103–16.

———. 1976. "Comments and Suggestions." *Social Problems* 24:40–41.

Gouldner, Helen. 2001. Interview with John F. Galliher. April 2.

Gross, Larry. 1993. *Contested Closets: The Politics and Ethics of Outing.* Minneapolis: University of Minnesota Press.

Harris, Fred R. 1970. Letter to the Honorable Omer Poos, December 21. One Institute and Archives.

Henslin, James M. 2001a. *Sociology: A Down to Earth Approach.* 5th ed. Boston: Allyn and Bacon.

———. 2001b. Interview with John F. Galliher, June 14.

———. 2001c. E-mail message to John F. Galliher, June 15.

Herman, Nancy J. 1993. "Return to Sender: Reintegrative Stigma-Management Strategies of Ex-Psychiatric Patients." *Journal of Contemporary Ethnography* 22:295–330.

Herman, Nancy J., and Gil Richard Musolf. 1998. "Resistance among Ex-Psychiatric Patients." *Journal of Contemporary Ethnography* 26:426–49.

Hess, Beth B., Elizabeth W. Markson, and Peter J. Stein. 1985. *Sociology.* 2nd ed. New York: Macmillan.

Hessler, Richard, and John F. Galliher. 1983. "Institutional Review Boards and Clandestine Research: An Empirical Test." *Human Organization* 42:82–86.

Hills, Frederic W. 1980. Letter to Theron Raines, September 9. One Institute and Archives.

Hoffman, Martin. 1971. Review of *Tearoom Trade. Archives of Sexual Behavior* 1: 98–100.

Hollister, John Walker. 2002. "Reconstructing Social Theory at a Cruising Site." Ph.D. diss., State University of New York, Binghamton.

Hoover, Eric. 2003. "Policing Public Sex." *Chronicle of Higher Education* 49 (January 17): A31.

Horowitz, Irving Louis. 1970. Letter to the Honorable Omer Poos, December 16. One Institute and Archives.

———. 1983. *C. Wright Mills: An American Utopian.* New York: Free Press.

————. 2001. Letter to John F. Galliher, October 3.

Horowitz, Irving Louis, and Lee Rainwater. 1975. "Sociological Snoopers and Journalistic Moralizers, part 2." In Laud Humphreys, *Tearoom Trade: Impersonal Sex in Public Places*, Retrospect: 181–90 (Chicago: Aldine).

Horowitz, Ruth. 1986. "Remaining an Outsider: Membership as a Threat to Research Rapport." *Urban Life* 14:409–30.

Humphreys, Laud. n.d. "Letter to Dad." One Institute and Archives

————. n.d. Book Manuscript. One Institute and Archives.

————. 1968a. Letter to Robert Habenstein, September 11. One Institute and Archives.

————. 1968b. Letter to Mary Wise, November 26. One Institute and Archives.

————. 1969. Letter to John S. Rendleman, August 26. One Institute and Archives.

————. 1970a. *Tearoom Trade: Impersonal Sex in Public Places*. Chicago: Aldine.

————. 1970b. "Tearoom Trade: Impersonal Sex in Public Places.'" *Trans-action* (January): 10–25.

————. 1970c. "Jesus Christ: A Sexual Person?" *Vector* (December): 13, 14, 38.

————. 1971a. "New Styles in Homosexual Manliness." *Trans-action* (March/April): 38–46, 64–65.

————. 1971b. Letter to Lewis A. Coser, June 16. One Institute and Archives.

————. 1972a. Letter to Glenn Goodwin, January 18. One Institute and Archives.

————. 1972b. *Out of the Closets: The Sociology of Homosexual Liberation*. Englewood Cliffs, N.J.: Prentice Hall.

————. 1975. *Tearoom Trade: Impersonal Sex in Public Places. Enlarged Edition with a Retrospect on Ethical Issues*. Chicago: Aldine.

————. 1978. "An Interview with Evelyn Hooker." *Alternative Lifestyles* 1: 191–206.

————. 1979a. "Being Odd against All Odds." In Ronald C. Federico, *Sociology*, 2nd ed., 238–43 (Reading, Mass.: Addison-Wesley).

————. 1979b. "Exodus and Identity: The Emerging Gay Culture," In *Gay Men: The Sociology of Male Homosexuality*, ed. Martin P. Levin, 134–47 (New York: Harper and Row).

————. 1980a. Letter to Theron Raines, July 30. One Institute and Archives.

————. 1980b. Review of *Homosexuality in Perspective*. *Trans-action* (September/October): 84–86.

————. 1985. Letter to Acting Dean Donald Brenneis, May 3. In the possession of John F. Galliher.

Humphreys, Laud, and Brian Miller. 1980. "Identities in the Emerging Gay Culture." In *Homosexual Behavior: A Modern Reappraisal*, ed. Judd Marmor, 147–57 (New York: Basic Books).

Hunter, Herbert M., and Sameer Y. Abraham, eds. 1987. *Race, Class, and the World System: The Sociology of Oliver C. Cox.* New York: Monthly Review.

Jaarsma, Sjoerd R. 2002. "Ownership and Control of Ethnographic Materials." *Anthropology News* (October): 17.

Jagose, Annamarie. 1996. *Queer Theory: An Introduction.* New York: New York University Press.

Jones, James H. 1993. *Bad Blood: The Tuskegee Syphilis Experiment.* New York: Free Press.

Jones, Vern. 2001. Interview with John F. Galliher, April 7.

————. 2003. E-mail message to John F. Galliher, October 24.

Kancelbaum, Barbara. 2002. "Social Scientists and Institutional Review Boards." *Items and Issues* 3:1–5.

Karp, David A. 1973. "Hiding in Pornographic Bookstores: A Reconsideration of the Nature of Urban Anonymity." *Urban Life* 1:427–51.

————. 1992. "Illness Ambiguity and the Search for Meaning: A Case Study of a Self-Help Group for Affective Disorders." *Journal of Contemporary Ethnography* 21:139–70.

Kelman, Herbert C. 1982. "Ethical Issues in Different Social Science Methods." In *Ethical Issues in Social Science Research,* ed. Tom L. Beauchamp, Ruth R. Faden, R. Jay Wallace Jr., and Leroy Walters, 40–98 (Baltimore, Md.: The Johns Hopkins University Press).

Keys, David P., and John F. Galliher. 2000. *Confronting the Drug Control Establishment: Alfred Lindesmith as a Public Intellectual.* Albany: State University of New York Press.

Koffler, Richard [Executive Editor at Aldine de Gruyter]. 2003. Letter to John F. Galliher, January 2.

Kornblum. William. 2000. *Sociology in a Changing World.* 5th ed. Fort Worth: Harcourt.

LaPiere, Richard T. 1934. "Attitudes versus Action." *Social Forces* 13:230–37.

Lavin, David E. 1971. Review of *Tearoom Trade. Annuals of the American Academy of Political and Social Science* 398:199–200.

Lazere, Arthur. 1987. "Laud Humphreys: Monday, Bloody Monday." *New York Native* (June 8): 16. One Institute and Archives.

Lee, John Alan. 1979. "The Gay Connection." *Urban Life* 8:175–98.

Leo, Richard A. 1995 "Trial and Tribulations: Courts, Ethnography, and the Need for an Evidentiary Privilege of Academic Researchers." *American Sociologist* 26:113–34.

Lesser Feasts and Fasts, 2000. 2001. New York: Church Publishing.

Liebow, Elliot. 1967. *Tally's Corner.* Boston: Little, Brown.

Lilly, J. Robert, and Richard A. Ball. 1981. "No-Tell Motel: The Management of Social Invisibility." *Urban Life* 10:179–98.

Lindsey, Linda L., and Stephen Beach. 2002. *Sociology.* 2nd ed. Upper Saddle River, N.J.: Prentice Hall.

Lindesmith, Alfred R. 1947. *Opiate Addiction*. Bloomington, Ind.: Principia.

Lynch, Fred. 2001a. E-mail message to John F. Galliher, March 26.

―――――. 2001b. Interview with John F. Galliher, June 26.

Lynd, Robert S., and Helen Merrell Lynd. 1929. *Middletown: A Study in Contemporary American Culture*. New York: Harcourt, Brace.

Marx, Gary T. 1990. "Reflections on Academic Success and Failure: Making It, Forsaking It, Reshaping It." In *Authors of Their Own Lives: Intellectual Autobiographies by Twenty American Sociologists*, ed. Bennett M. Berger, 260-84 (Berkeley: University of California Press).

Mathes, Irma Bendel. 1966. "Adult Male Homosexuality and Perception of Instrumentality, Expressiveness, and Coalition in Parental Role Structure." Ph.D. diss., Missouri University-Columbia.

Middlemist, R. Dennis, Eric S. Knowles, and Charles F. Matter. 1976. "Personal Space Invasions in the Lavatory: Suggestive Evidence for Arousal." *Journal of Personality and Social Psychology* 33:541-46.

Mileski, Maureen, and Donald J. Black. 1972. "The Social Organization of Homosexuality." *Urban Life* 1:187-202.

Milgram, Stanley. 1974. *Obedience to Authority: An Experimental Test*. New York: Harper and Row.

Miller, Brian. 1982. "A Scholarly Taxi to the Toilets." *The Advocate* (April 15): 39-40.

―――――. 2001a. Letter to John F. Galliher, April 1.

―――――. 2001b. Interview with John F. Galliher, April 13.

Miller, Brian, and Laud Humphreys. 1980a. "Keeping in Touch: Maintaining Contact with Stigmatized Subjects." In *Fieldwork Experience: Qualitative Approaches to Social Research*, ed. William B. Shaffer, Robert A. Stebbins, and Allan Turowetz, 212-23 (New York: St. Martin's).

―――――. 1980b. "Lifestyles and Violence: Homosexual Victims of Assault and Murder." *Qualitative Sociology* 3:169-85.

Mitchell, John. 2001. Interview with John F. Galliher, March 25.

Nardi, Peter M. 1995. "'The Breastplate of Righteousness' Twenty-five Years after Laud Humphreys' *Tearoom Trade:* Impersonal Sex in Pubic Places." *Journal of Homosexuality* 30:1-10.

Nicolaus, Martin. 1969. "Remarks at ASA Convention." *American Sociologist* 4: 154-56.

New York Times. 1968. "Sociology Professor Accused of Beating Student," June 10, 25.

―――――. 1975. "Crimes against Homosexuals Analyzed," September 17, 14.

―――――. 2003a. "Strom Thurmond, Senate Institution Who Fought Integration, Dies at 100," June 28, 13.

―――――. 2003b. "Final Word: 'My Father's Name Was James Strom Thurmond,'" December 17, 1.

New York Times Magazine. 2000. "A Sinister Rorschach: Black Marks on the Freedom of Information," May 14, 27.

NIMH [National Institute of Mental Health]. 1968. "Report of Investigating Committee," July 31.

Oxford Dictionary of the Christian Church. 1974. Edited by F. L. Cross and E. A. Livingston. Oxford: Oxford University Press.

Pittman, David J. 2001. Letter to John F. Galliher, August 7.

Pitzer College. 1981. Five-Year Report on Laud Humphreys. In the possession of the authors.

Plummer, Ken. 1999. "The 'Ethnographic Society' at Century's End." *Journal of Contemporary Ethnography* 28:641–49.

Polsky, Ned. 1967. *Hustlers, Beats, and Others.* Chicago: Aldine.

————. 1970. "C. Wright Mills Award Committee Announcement." *Social Problems* 18.

Popenoe, David. 2000. *Sociology.* 11th ed. Upper Saddle River, N.J.: Prentice Hall.

Putney, Snell W. and Marvyn L. Cadwallader. 1957. "An Experiment in Crisis Interaction." In *Readings in Sociology,* ed. Robert O'Brien, Clarence Schrag, and Walter Martin, 40–44 (Boston: Houghton Mifflin); originally in *Research Studies of the State College of Washington* 22 (June 1954).

Rainwater, Lee. 1970. Letter to the Honorable Omer Poos, December 16. One Institute and Archives.

————. 2001. E-mail message to John F. Galliher, June 7.

Rainwater, Lee, and David J. Pittman. 1967. "Ethical Problems in Studying a Politically Sensitive Community." *Social Problems* 14:357–66.

Reisman, David, Nathan Glazer, and Reuel Denney. 1961. *The Lonely Crowd: A Study of American Character.* Garden City, N.Y.: Doubleday.

Reiss, Albert J., Jr. 1961. "The Social Integration of Queers and Peers." *Social Problems* 9:102–20.

Reiss, Ira L. 1971. Review of *Tearoom Trade. American Sociological Review* 36: 581–83.

Rendleman, John S. 1970. Letter to the Honorable Omer Poos, November 13. One Institute and Archives.

Reynolds, Paul Davidson 1983 "Commentary on 'Institutional Review Boards and Clandestine Research: An Experimental Test.'" *Human Organization* 42:87–89.

Rhudy, Rob. 2001. Interview with John F. Galliher, April 7.

Robertson, Ian. 1987. *Sociology.* 3rd ed. New York: Worth.

Rodrìguez Rust, Paula C. 2000. "Criticisms of the Scholarly Literature on Sexuality for Its Neglect of Bisexuality." In *Bisexuality in the United States: A Social Science Reader,* 5–10 (New York: Columbia University Press).

Russo, Anthony, and Laud Humphreys. 1983. "Homosexuality and Crime." In *Encyclopedia of Crime and Justice,* ed. Sanford H. Kadish, 866–72 (New York: Free Press).

Rust, Paula. 1996. "Monogamy and Polyamory: Relationship Issues for Bisexuals." In *The Psychology and Politics of an Invisible Minority,* ed. Beth A. Firestein, 127–48 (Thousand Oaks, Calif.: Sage).

Sagarin, Edward. 1974. "Homosexuality and the Homosexual: An Overview of the Former and a Denial of the Reality of the Latter." Paper read at the Meetings of the American Sociological Association, Montreal, August 26. One Institute and Archives.

Scarce, Rik. 1995. "Scholarly Ethics and Courtroom Antics: Where Researchers Stand in the Eyes of the Law." *American Sociologist* 26:87–112.

_____. 2001. Comments Made at a Plenary Session on Laud Humphreys at the Meetings of the Society for the Study of Social Problems, Anaheim, Calif., August 18.

Schacht, Steven P. 2001. "The Continued Personal and Professional Perils and Promise of Doing Same-Sex Research: Things Have to Change an Awful Lot to Stay the Same." Paper read at the Annual Meetings of the Society for the Study of Social Problems, Anaheim, Calif., August 18.

Schuessler, Karl. 2001. Interview with John F. Galliher, March 24.

Schwartz, Albert. 2001. Interview with John F. Galliher, April 25.

Schwartz, Richard D., and Jerome H. Skolnick. 1962. "Two Studies of Legal Stigma." *Social Problems* 10:133–42.

Scott, Barbara Marliene, and Mary Ann Schwartz. 2000. *Sociology: Making Sense of the Social World.* Boston: Allyn and Bacon.

Sedgwick, Eve Kosofsky. 1990. *Epistemology of the Closet.* Berkeley: University of California Press.

Seidman, Steven, ed. 1996. Introduction to *Queer Theory/Sociology,* 1–29 (Cambridge, Mass.: Blackwell).

Sewell, William T. 1970. Letter to the Honorable Omer Poos, December 15. One Institute and Archives.

Shepard, Jon M. 2002. *Sociology.* 8th ed. Belmont, Calif.: Wadsworth.

Shover, Neal. 1975. "Tarnished Goods and Services in the Marketplace." *Urban Life* 3:471–88.

Shulman, David. 1994. "Dirty Data and Investigative Methods." *Journal of Contemporary Ethnography* 23:214–53.

Smith , Dusky Lee. 2001. Interview with John F. Galliher, April 10.

Southern Illinois University Police Report. 1969. August 14. One Institute and Archives.

Sprow, Allen J. 1970. Review of *Tearoom Trade. Library Journal* 95:2704.

St. Louis Globe-Democrat. 1968a. "Student-Professor Fight at W.U. Called Infantile," June 12, 11A. One Institute and Archives.

_____. 1968b. "W.U. Magazine Loses Subsidy, Hikes Price," July 5, 8A. One Institute and Archives.

_____. 1968c. "W.U. Furor: Homosexual Study a Major Factor," July 18, 1A. One Institute and Archives.

_____. 1968d. "U.S. Team to Visit W.U. in Grant Controversy," July 19, 3A. One Institute and Archives.

St. Louis Post Dispatch. 1968. "Eliot Denies Charges by Seven Sociologists," July18, 16A.

Stromberg, Ann. 2001. Interview with John F. Galliher, May 16.

Student Life. 1968a. "Protest Prevents Dow from Recruiting Here," February 16, 1.

_____. 1968b. "Turmoil Thrives in Sociology Dept.," September 20, 1, 11, 14.

Styles, Joseph. 1979. "Outsider/Insider Researching Gay Baths." *Urban Life* 8: 135-52.

Sullivan, Mortimer A., Jr., Stuart A. Queen, and Ralph C. Patrick Jr. 1958. "Participant Observation as Employed in the Study of a Military Training Program." *American Sociological Review* 23:660-67.

Sullivan, Thomas J. 2001. *Sociology: Concepts and Applications in a Diverse World.* Boston: Allyn and Bacon.

Sundholm, Charles A. 1973. "The Pornographic Arcade: Ethnographic Notes on Moral Men in Immoral Places." *Urban Life* 2:85-104.

Taylor, Laurie. 1970. "Cottage Queens" [review of *Tearoom Trade*]. *New Society* (London), November 5. One Institute and Archives.

Taylor, Verta, and Nicole C. Raeburn. 1995. "Identity Politics as High-Risk Activism: Career Consequences for Lesbian, Gay, and Bisexual Sociologists." *Social Problems* 42:252-73.

Thompson, William E., and Joseph V. Hickey. 1999. *Society in Focus: An Introduction to Sociology.* New York: Longman.

Tittle, Charles R., and Alan R. Rowe. 1973. "Moral Appeal, Sanction Threat, and Deviance: An Experimental Test." *Social Problems* 20:488-98.

Toch, Hans. 2001. Interview with John F. Galliher, June 18.

Tulsa Tribune. 1960. "Parties Continue for Miss Nancy Wallace," August 20.

Turner, William B. 2000. *A Genealogy of Queer Theory.* Philadelphia: Temple University Press.

United States Court of Appeals for the Seventh Circuit. 1972. *U.S. v. Robert Allan Laud Humphreys,* No. 71-1137, 457.2d 242; 1972 App. Lexis 11096, February 25.

United States Department of Health, Education, and Welfare. 1973. "Final Report of the Tuskegee Syphilis Study Ad Hoc Advisory Panel." Washington, D.C: U.S. Government Printing Office.

United States District Court, Southern District of Illinois. 1970-1972, *U.S. v. Humphreys,* No. 7002.

Volti, Rudi. 2001. Interview with John F. Galliher, April 30.

Von den Hoonard, Will C. 2001. "In Research-Ethics Review a Moral Panic?" *Canadian Review of Sociology and Anthropology* 38:19-36.

von Hoffman, Nicholas. 1975. "Sociological Snoopers and Journalistic Moralizers, part 1." In Laud Humphreys, *Tearoom Trade: Impersonal Sex in Public Places,* Retrospect: 177-81 (Chicago: Aldine).

Warren, Carol A. B. 1980. "Data Presentation and the Audience: Responses, Ethics, and Effects." *Urban Life* 9:282–308.

Warren, Carol A. B., and Joannn S. DeLora. 1978. "Student Protest in the 1970s: The Gay Student Union and the Military." *Urban Life* 7:67–90.

Warwick, Donald P. 1975a. "Tearoom Trade: Means and Ends in Social Research." In Laud Humphreys, *Tearoom Trade: Impersonal Sex in Public Places*, Retrospect: 191–212 (Chicago: Aldine).

————. 1975b. "Social Scientists Ought to Stop Lying." *Psychology Today*, February, 38, 40, 105–6.

Washington Post. 1999. "Hate May Have Triggered Fatal Barracks Beating; Slain Soldier Had Been Taunted on Base as Secret Emerged about His Sexuality," August 11, A1.

Washington University. n.d. "Grievances of the Graduate Students of the Department of Sociology." One Institute and Archives.

————. 1968a. Memo from the Faculty and Graduate Student Union, May 16. One Institute and Archives.

————. 1968b. Final Doctor of Philosophy Examination of Robert Allan Laud Humphreys, May 16.

————. 1968c. Letter to Chancellor Thomas H. Eliot from Some Tenured Faculty, Sociology Department, May 24.

————. 1968d. "University Sells Social Science Magazine to Academic Corporation." *Alumni News* (September). One Institute and Archives.

Weinberg, Martin. 1974. Review of *Out of the Closets. Contemporary Sociology* 3: 263–66.

Whyte, William Foote. 1955. *Street Corner Society*. Chicago: University of Chicago Press.

Wiens, Arthur N. 1971. Review of *Tearoom Trade. Contemporary Psychology* 16: 430–32.

Wilkins, Leslie T. 1970. Letter to the Honorable Omer Poos, December 17. One Institute and Archives.

Wilson, William Julius. 1987. *The Truly Disadvantaged: The Inner City, the Underclass, and Public Policy*. Chicago: University of Chicago Press.

————. 1996. *When Work Disappears: The World of the New Urban Poor*. New York: Knopf.

Yancy, William. 2001a. Interview with John F. Galliher, February 20.

————. 2001b. E-mail message to John F. Galliher, May 22.

Zimbardo, Philip G. 1972. "Comment: Pathology of Imprisonment." *Society* (April): 4, 6, 8.

Zimmerman, Don H., and D. Lawrence Wieder. 1977. "The Diary: Diary Interview Method." *Urban Life* 5:479–98.

Index